TAPESTRY OF CREATION

RACHEL WHITE

Revive your primal and divine creativity to make your entire life your greatest work of art

TAPESTRY OF CREATION

RACHEL WHITE

Copyright © 2023 Rachel White
Mildura, Australia

This book may not be reproduced, in its entirety or any portion, in any form, without the explicit written consent from the publisher Rachel White. All rights reserved.

Paperback ISBN: 978-0-6456064-3-0
eBook ISBN: 978-0-6456064-4-7

Imprint: Independently Published

For your evolution, your art, and for the creative force of life wanting to experience itself through you.

CONTENTS

INTRODUCTION	11
CHAPTER ONE	
YOUR CREATIVE IMPULSE	15
Your life-force is your creative energy	17
Imitate, innovate, invent: a path to discovering your creative style	21
Make *your* moves from the vision YOU can see	29
Ideas are like energetic butterflies that love whispering into your ear	33
Your creations are MAGIC and MEDICINE	39
Create for yourself first	41
Alchemising the fear of making a mistake and overcoming the inevitable case of imposter syndrome	43
It's meant to feel easy	53
Your creative impulse: summary	59
CHAPTER TWO	
THE WORLD AS YOUR MUSE	61
The gentle approach to romanticising life	63
Contemplation – a portal to revelation	67
Alchemise intimidation into inspiration	70
Infusing artfulness into the mundane	73
The power of contrast and staying in motion	76
In a world you could create anything, how to choose what ideas you follow.	79
Creating your own signs from the universe	83
See the art above, below, and within	86
Wouldn't it be great if…?	87
Honouring the roots	90
Don't take life too seriously	92
The world as your muse: summary	94

CHAPTER THREE
YOUR CREATIVE TEMPO   95

Your natural rhythm + divine synchronicity   97
Creativity expands time, btw - time isn't linear   100
The Alpha State   106
When you are ahead of your time   108
Sacred laziness – allowing what you do to be enough 113
Be your own gatekeeper   118
The flow of your evolution   121
Disruption to your rhythm   123
The dance of your action   126
There is no rush – spaciousness   128
Extend your breath to extend your life   133
Your creative tempo: summary   135

CHAPTER FOUR
WOMB WISDOM   137

13 drops of wisdom from the womb   139
1. Breathe before anything else   141
2. Sacred boundaries   142
3. The duality and union of creation: masculine and
feminine energy   144
4. Inner seasons of life   146
5. Beauty in the void   148
6. Your sexual energy, creative energy, and life-force
are all one in the same   151
7. Prosperity is your birthright   153
8. Your emotions are divine signals   155
9. The pulse of your clit is guiding you into a deeper
flow with life   156
10. Your darkness is sacred   157
11. The sacred ancestry   Part of you existed within
your grandmother's womb.   160
12. The parallels between the creation of; human life
and creative life   162

13. You hold so much more depth than you are raised
in this world to believe — 170
Womb wisdom: summary — 172

CHAPTER FIVE
THE JOURNEY THROUGH YOUR BODY — 173

Crown – the divine channel — 176
Third Eye – the wonder of the worlds — 178
Throat – the activated voice — 180
Heart – the sacred bridge — 182
Solar Plexus – the confident power — 185
Sacral – the sensual sea — 191
Root – the grounded foundation — 192
The journey through your body: summary — 194

CHAPTER SIX
THE DEPTHS OF BEING HUMAN — 195

The spectrum of being human — 197
Emotions and their influence on your creative expression — 200
How your pain can fuel your art — 209
The embodiment of your depth — 213
How your depth informs your art — 215
The depths of being human: summary — 217

CHAPTER SEVEN
LIBERATION THROUGH CREATION — 219

Liberation is provoking you — 221
Liberate yourself from your past work — 223
Liberate yourself from the dreams of others — 226
Liberate your voice — 228
Re-wild your inner child — 232
Your heroic journey — 235
Your multi-dimensional nature — 238
Creation as a spiritual practice — 240
There can be no liberation, without your creative energy. — 242

Liberation through creation: summary — 244

CHAPTER EIGHT
YOU ARE A WORK OF ART — 245

Differentiated through unity — 247
The divine drama of your life — 250
Drivers of your artful character development — 253
Interweaving storylines — 255
The script of life — 257
Living in the moment — 260
Curating your inner art gallery — 261
Life as poetry — 263
The greatest story ever told — 265
You are a work of art: summary — 267

FINAL WORDS — 268

ACKNOWLEDGMENTS — 271
ABOUT THE AUTHOR — 274
REFERENCES — 277

INTRODUCTION

You are creative because you exist – this is a message I invite you to keep front of mind as you journey through each page of this book. You were born with creative energy inside of you, sending impulses through your body calling you to create.

It is creativity itself that brings art and beauty into the world, creating a forever lasting cycle where each creation is a musing that engenders more creation to be born.

This book is a collection of 74 short essays that together create a tapestry of the many elements to making your life the artful experience it ought to be, woven together by the common thread of your creative impulse. Each builds on the last while weaving into each other, the sections of the tapestry are broken up into the different chapters exploring different overarching themes.

While I was growing up, I formed the belief that I wasn't creative, I wasn't 'good' at anything that we generally attribute to 'professional artists' like painters, singers, and so forth. As I grew older, I came to realise how innovative I was and began to see my ability to attract ideas and swiftly move forward into action to bring those ideas to life. When I started to redefine what I thought it meant to be a creative person I started to see just how creativity ran through the veins of every single person in existence.

Even though we are all creative beings, the relationship we have with our creative energy influences how we creatively express and bring our art into the world.

When I started expressing myself more, in a way that embraced my flavour of creativity, there were moments of imposter syndrome and self-doubt. Feeling like I didn't belong with the 'creatives' who have been into writing or other forms of art for their entire lives. Like I didn't meet their standards or rules. But as I allowed myself to keep expressing, I found my own space to keep creating and allowing each piece of my art to be perfect for the moment it was created in.

The more I created in this way, the more I realised that our creative energy expands far beyond the tangible art we produce. Our creative energy is infused into every single facet of our life, from the way we breathe, to the way we sweep the floor, drive to the supermarket, speak to our lover, run our business or do our work, and the way we live the storyline of our life.

This book was written from the perspective of someone who had to revive, redefine, and reclaim their full creative expression as an adult. I didn't pursue artistry in what you may define in a traditional sense.

There can be just as much art in the way someone plays a game of tennis, to the best book in the world, to the way you wash your dishes on a random Tuesday night. Some moments and expressions of art may seem bigger than others, but when we zoom out at the cosmic storyline of creation, all are just tiny moments within the interconnected web of interweaving and overlapping storylines.

As you move through this book you will explore –

• Just how sacred your creative impulse is and how to fully reconnect with this sacred part of your inner world.
• That the world is your muse to find inspiration and art in, to fuel your own inspired state of mind. How playfulness

and taking life less seriously makes way for your art to flow through you with great ease.

- Tuning into the divine tempo of your creativity and how this connects you to the rhythm of the universe, where divine synchronicity is commonplace through your life.
- The sacred codes and lessons your womb holds about creation and life. The womb we explore here is your energetic womb and the cosmic womb.
- How creative ideas take an energetic journey through your body in preparation to be born into the world.
- The spectrum of your human existence and how your primal emotions, pleasure, pain, and all that you experience is sacred fuel for your art.
- Liberation and freedom through your creativity.
- How your life is your greatest work of art.

Each component of this book builds on the next, but your journey (and your life) is not linear so you can choose to explore in whatever way you feel inspired and drawn to.

There is cross over between different chapters. There are contradictions and paradoxes.

The most beautiful paradox is that everything matters, *and* nothing matters. You apply the meaning you resonate with from all that you explore. There is so much depth, nuance, and complexities, *and* everything has a simple essence.

There is a lot of magic.

And there is some mess.

There are some parts of this book that perhaps leave more questions than answers. This is the fun part for you to trust how your divine wisdom fills in the gaps and how your mind plays with the ideas that I am putting forward.

Some of my biggest muses for writing this book were Taylor Swift, The Gene Keys by Richard Rudd, and Nature itself. You will see many references to these creators along with many more throughout your journey in this book. In this way the References section can also be viewed as a suggested resources page. All of my inspiration and muses are part of the tapestry within this book and through my life.

Take everything you read as something to contemplate and muse with as an entry point to connect with your own inner wisdom. Take nothing as gospel, or too seriously.

As you move through the pages and chapters keep reminding yourself that you are creative because you exist.

CHAPTER ONE
YOUR CREATIVE IMPULSE

You are creative beyond any measure; your essence is designed to express sacred art and treasure. Your style is unique, unable to compare; play in your journey of creating with the world to share.

Sacred Symbolism – the butterfly

The codes of the butterfly are held within the cells of the caterpillar. The caterpillar lives its life with its sacred evolution pre-determined. The caterpillar is born to transform into a butterfly, just as you are born to evolve into your most creative and full self.

The caterpillar consumes and consumes, just as you consume the world around you through information and experiences.

The caterpillar consumes until one day it just can't take anymore in, it hangs up-side-down and begins spinning its sacred space for isolation and transformation, its cocoon. As one day you too will arrive at a point of being unnourished from the external information you have been consuming and will turn inwards to seek your own inner wisdom.

Within the cocoon the caterpillar begins a gruesome death, digesting itself, turning into an oozing goo. The cells that survive this process are the ones that hold the coding for the butterfly's eyes, wings, legs, and all other parts. All of these cells the caterpillar was born with, predetermining it to live this story of evolution. The cells of the butterfly take in the ooze to grow the butterfly. When ready, the cocoon cracks open and the butterfly emerges. Just as you will metaphorically break parts of yourself down, the parts that have no place in the next chapter of your evolution, you see the sacred parts of yourself that you were born with, and rebuild your external identity up, using all of who you were to shape the rebirthed version. The butterfly holds all the memories of the caterpillar, nothing from the previous moments in your story are ever wasted.

The butterfly takes flight. Liberated in the world.

The codes of your creative evolution are codes you were born with. Your creative path is equally divine and primal, just as it is for the butterfly.

The symbolic journey of rebirth plays out many times within one human life. It is the depth already coded within you that will ultimately liberate you, be willing to follow the creative impulse from deep within yourself that is driving your evolution, your story, and your artful experience of life.

Are you willing to fly as your inner butterfly?

Your life-force is your creative energy

Your life-force energy, creative energy, and sexual energy are all one in the same. They all come from the same power source. Our creative energy is innate within us. It is our life-force. When we tune into this truth, it is evident that we are all creative. Regardless of how creative you think you are, or how creative other people told you, you were or were not growing up, you were born creative.

Any definition for what you think it means to be creative, outside of simply being alive, throw it in the bin and delete it from your mindset right now to continue your journey through this book with the blank canvas of a beginner's mind.

Being creative means that you have a capacity to create, as long as you have a life-force, as long as you are breathing, you have an innate impulse that drives you to create. You will have this impulse until you have your last breath when your body no longer has a life-force flowing through it.

Your life-force energy is what animates your body. A human being born into the world becomes animated with life through their first birth. As soon as the baby takes its first birth, they become alive for their life of creation on earth. It is our breath that allows us to live in the world, to interact, procreate and co-create. As our life-force becomes activated by our first breath, so does our primal impulse to create. To continue life, to evolve life.

We are creating in every moment, of every day. We create with our thoughts alone, our thoughts can create new states of being within ourselves, and drive us to take action that changes the inner and outer state of others. Our thoughts and actions create many ripples of impact and consequences through our creative impulses when we are living our daily life, completing mundane tasks. It is our creative impulse that starts new points of the *butterfly effect*, where small changes can ripple in large changes. Our actions can build, they can destroy, they can alchemise by transforming one form into another. Our actions can innovate and imitate. It is our creative impulse, our innate inner impulse, that drives us to create new states of being through our lives and the world. This all plays out in every moment at a subconscious and energetic level.

If this is the power your creative impulse has when you are not even paying attention to it, imagine what could happen when you harness that energy?

Energy is all around us, to be played with, to be created into new things with. We have a primal drive that pulls us and draws us into the energy that is for us to play with.

Your creative energy is both primal and divine.

You are so fucking creative.

You are SO creative, take a moment to own this powerful truth.

If you stop reading this book after Chapter One that is ok, as long as you take this message and truly believe that you are an insanely creative person, purely because you exist.

Right now, revisit your mindset, if there is any shred of a belief that tells you that you are not creative, or you are not as creative as other people, or you can't be creative because (fill in bullshit reason here) – throw all of it out! It is all bullshit! There is no way in this world for you to not be a creative person!

Ok, now that, that rubbish is in the bin, take a moment to reflect on all the things you have created in your life. You have created within every conversation you have had, you have created within every relationship that you have had, maybe you have created a literal human being inside of you, or helped co-create one, if you have raised a child you have co-created many parts of them that live on, you have created your home, likely many things within your home, if you have a business you have created so much through your products and services, if you work in services you have created so much in the form of solutions and much more. You have created millions of moments and more in your home, work, and everyday life. You create in every moment; you just can't help it! Being creative is about so much more than painting, drawing, performing, and all the monetised creative endeavours that we often grow up associating being creative with. And it also includes all of those things that can enrich our lives if we feel drawn to those crafts. We create ALL the time; we can make art out of our everyday life. We do make art out of everyday life, with our primal creative energy.

We are naturally creative; we always have our creative impulse creating something. When we harness this energy in the direction we choose, we become literal magic makers. You will amaze yourself with what you can do with the primal gifts within your body.

Tune into this truth again – you are SO creative.

You have such a high capacity to create in such a beautiful way. Go out and make magic!

Within your creative energy, and creative expression, lies extraordinary depth. This is your invitation and permission slip to go and explore, and to feel the expansiveness inside of you when you engage with this innate field of energy.

For as long as you have a pulse, for as long as you are breathing, every single thing you create is a work of art if you choose to see it as such. This isn't something that adds pressure, your art is allowed to capture all of what exudes life – the mess, the mundane, the mystery, the madness, and the magic.

Take a moment in reverence to your innate creative power before moving forward to the next part of this chapter.

Imitate, innovate, invent: a path to discovering your creative style

Your unique creative style may feel a little intimidating when you first begin thinking about it and playing with what exactly it will look like. The pressure to create something completely original from the very beginning can dilute the potency of your invention before you even allow yourself to get started. The gentle path with less resistance is to begin with imitation, then move into innovation, and you will naturally arrive at invention with your own creative style.

You subconsciously have been following this path your entire life. Look at the development of most children, most of their actions are modelled on what they see happening around them, they imitate. Through their play, they naturally innovate, they add things together, they try something new and like how it works, and then all of a sudden, something completely new emerges from their play in an invention of their own leaving the adults wondering where that thing their kid did or said even came from.

This invention likely still carries elements of their imitation and innovation, but it is fresh in the way it carries their unique style. This process is natural for children because they do not have their mind chiming in trying to convince them that they cannot be innovative or inventive, or that there is no 'point' to their play.

When you don't think about, you are a natural at this process too. The things we think the most about, are the things we make much more complicated than they could be, and the more we think about it the more our creative energy becomes diluted around this creative idea/project. The problem is that it is often the things we care the most about that we think about the most.

Give yourself the grace and patience to play with the process of intimation, innovation, and invention, to explore and embrace your own creative style.

Imitation – modelling the actions and expression we see others performing. This can be in all kinds ways through all realms of life.

When a child who loves to sing first learns this form of expression, they will often imitate the singers that they love or the adults in their life they see and hear singing. They will sing their songs, attempting to emulate the magic and style of their inspiration. We can see in some artists now where their inspiration came from and the last generation of singers they grew up singing along to, that inspiration is still infused within the invention of their own style that they have arrived at now. Some may still be in their innovation phase where the original is very obvious even when they have added their own flare.

When you are exploring something new that you want to play in the field of with your creative energy, whether it is through singing, drawing, business, writing, gardening, any skill at all, you can apply this to any new pursuit that you desire to do, or any project you want to bring to life, anything you want to create. You can begin with imitation.

When it comes to doing something brand new, something you have never tried before, your body will feel a level of fear as you embark on a path full of unknown terrain, you can tune into this fear as an invitation for expansion, rather than listening to the mind's interpretation of the fear and allowing it to tell you that you are not capable of doing this new thing and even worse believing your mind when it says these things. There will always be a degree of fear and discomfort in the body when you are doing or even just exploring something new, you can let it hold you back or you can choose to roll with it. To invite some comfort into your transition, know that you can learn through imitating others.

Imitating doesn't mean to copy other people and then monetise it straight away, it doesn't mean to steal or undermine the work or creativity of others, you get to choose your own integrity lines here with your intention behind your imitation.

Some examples for me are from when I started getting into drawing and painting throughout 2021, this impulse came about when I started writing some kids books. The writing part felt really easy and flowed very effortlessly, the imagery wasn't as effortless and I wanted it to match the magic of the words. Being around my nephew and little cousins at the time meant I was seeing a lot of kids books and the amazing illustrations within them, my sneaky mind was telling me that my art could never be as good, but I chose to believe other wise and know that whatever I created would be *my* work of art. I had never really given myself the opportunity to develop the skill of drawing outside of little scribbles in the margin of many workbooks and journals, so I begun with imitation. The two things I begun doing through my imitation phase was paying a lot more attention when looking at kids books to the illustrations, how they were placed, laid out, the styles and elements that I liked, and I also spent a lot of time just googling different images of illustrations for elements I wanted to include in my kids books, I would copy parts into my sketchbook, through that alone I really impressed myself with how they ended up. These images that I copied never ended up inside my books or shared publicly, but imitating them for my own practice really increased my confidence, and my awareness around what style of drawing I liked doing.

This step of imitation can be used in business and our work life too. If you have had any training, in coaching, yoga, accounting, teaching, any area at all, you will likely begin by imitating a lot of what was taught to you. The language your teachers used and the way they phrased or explained things, the processes and structures you were taught, all of this is imitation and is a natural beginning step.

When imitating in the beginning of your business you may imitate the way you see others that you follow post on social media, or the way they launch their offers, or run their programs. Again it is up to you to draw your line of integrity. There may be times where you deem it necessary to credit your inspiration, or to show appreciation for their influence in some way. There are times when imitating the surface or structural elements of another's business are ok, but I would say that imitating their content or depth of their messaging is never ok – unless you are crediting them as the source and then adding on, or asking them for permission when appropriate. Through playing with your delivery of what you have imitated you will naturally move into innovation.

Innovation – after your solid foundation and understanding, you begin to build on that foundation by adding your unique flare, adding and merging different elements and integrating more of you into your creations.

Innovation is adding value to something existing. This may be in the form of a new business offer that you run differently to your last one by adding in and taking things out of your imitated first version. You may adjust an existing project. Our creative impulse drives us to improve upon our creations so that new life is constantly flowing through. You may innovate with the inventions of others too, adding value to the foundation they have built. Through your innovation you begin to intertwine your creative flair with your art, but there is still much of the old structure or foundation left so it isn't quite a unique invention of your own yet. This doesn't make it less valuable at the time, it is just another step in the natural evolution of your artistry.

Invention – your completely unique creative style expressed and manifested in the world.

Your unique inventions can still carry hints of inspiration from others at times, but they are birthed from your originality, from your own depth. It is something that came directly from you.

Your inventions make way for your creative style and expression to be transmitted throughout the world. Some of your inventions may not need you to go through the first two steps of imitating and innovating first, some will spontaneously emerge from the core of your being, other inventions may be building up in energy for decades, being fueled by any different creative imitations and innovations all combined. Often it takes patience and trust to fully discover your unique creative expression and how to harness that into your inventions.

You may find that you prefer to only innovate, to add value to what others create, the way you do this may capture your inventiveness. This is not a linear path. Like life, your creativity flows in spirals.

Your unique creative expression can never truly be imitated in a way that infuses your creative spirit into the art. You do not need to worry about others copying you from an energetic level. Even when you imitate others throughout your journey, you are only imitating the surface and never the true depth.

What is it that you have felt pulled towards, but you have been holding yourself back from even beginning? Maybe it feels too hard, or your mind is telling you that you will never be good at it, so what is the point of even beginning? *(Side note – you do not need to be good at everything, not everything you create needs to be objectively 'good' either, creating for the pure joy of something is enough reason in and of itself.)* Often our mind creates resistance by telling us that this new thing will not be easy, it will be hard and the mind will fight against that potential discomfort because it knows that it is that very discomfort that expands us.

Breathe through the growing pains and invite ease into the learning period for anything new by giving yourself grace and patience to make mistakes, to feel fear, to be a little uncomfortable, to play and grow, and create at the same time.

Have fun by looking for inspiration, imitate it for your own personal learning, innovate if you feel called to and allow your unique style of creation to be invented from this process.

The more you lean into this with the intention to express your creative style into the world, the more turned on and up your creative energy becomes, the more effortless this process becomes and also the more efficient.

Until you have moved through this, the thought that you could invent something completely original will seem unrealistic. And it is unrealistic, until you tune into your own creative power and allow yourself to take the first step in the direction that you want to go.

An important caveat to this process of moving through imitation, innovation, to invention is to allow yourself to keep moving into new steps and layers. Staying in step one of imitation forever will not serve your creativity, expression, or sense of fulfilment and enjoyment in whatever you are doing. You don't need to hide behind imitation in fear that you won't arrive at your own style.

Imitation can become a shadow to hide in that leads to a life of mediocrity. As explored by Richard Rudd, in his book The Gene Keys: Embracing Your Higher Purpose, the transmission of the 8th Gene Key shares that "the fear of the 8th shadow, like all shadow frequencies, is founded upon a specific fear and in this case it is the fear of being different." The shadow of mediocrity keeps you from "thinking outside the box" and leads to you becoming "a part of the background of life rather than a major player." Richard Rudd goes on to say that "to break out of the heavyweight frequency of the 8th shadow you have to take an exciting leap of faith in yourself." The 8th Gift of Style is about "following your own unique rebellious spirit out into the world." Your unique style is the "flowering of your individuality." This can never be an imitation of another, nor can it be imitated by another. This gift within The Gene Keys is the "cutting edge of creation itself" and when individuals surrender to the process of creation this gift emerges.

It doesn't matter if you have this gene key active in your profile or not, each of the 64 Gene Keys are within the collective and have threads within us. If this is the first you are hearing of the gene keys, I am excited to be the one to give you little snippets of their magic throughout this book. If you are curious to explore more about the Gene Keys, I have many podcast episodes, YouTube videos, and social media posts exploring different facets of the transmission, and The Gene Keys books and website contain a beautiful ocean of information that you can explore.

Your unique style is full of "genius and quantum leaps" and it is part of the journey to finding it to travel through the shadow of trying to be like everybody else first. Unconsciously living in the shadow of imitation leads to a life of mediocrity. While being aware of the part of the story you are in and using the energy of imitation to bring you into flow with the next natural step unlocks the gifts of your innovation and invention, to create and live in your own unique style.

Make *your* moves from the vision YOU can see

During 2021 while staying with my Aunty and Uncle in their NSW coastal home, we were playing around with their virtual reality goggles and games. In the set up that they had, once you put on the goggles and set the parameters of your space, you could play all kinds of games, explore 360-degree imagery of places all around the world, and many other aspects that took you into the experience of somewhere different to where you physically were. It can make you feel as if you are on a rollercoaster simply by what you are seeing and hearing. Even though you are safely sitting on a chair, your body reacts and moves like you *are* in a different world.

When I was playing one of the games, it involved me going into this spaceship and choosing one of various challenges. The challenge I chose involved cubes flying towards me from all different directions and me using a lightsaber type of tool to slice them in half just before they reached me. The cubes were to my left, my right, and front on, and sometimes I had to duck or dodge to one side to miss something else hitting me. All of this to the beat of the song that was playing. To me this was a really fun game that I was completely immersed in. To my Aunty and Uncle watching me play, I looked crazy waving my arms around seemingly pointlessly, moving around and working up a sweat! Of course, it looked crazy to them, because they couldn't see what I was seeing. When I saw my Aunty freaking out about the rollercoaster she was virtually on, instead of the little hit of fear she was getting, I was just laughing at her reactions of 'Woah! Woah! Omg!!' If I was in that experience with her, I would have been freaking out too and having a completely different experience.

In both cases, each of us were only reacting and responding to the vision we could see, allowing ourselves to immerse in that reality for that moment. It didn't matter that there was someone laughing on the couch two steps away from me not understanding why I was doing what I was doing. It didn't matter that I couldn't feel the fear of being on the rollercoaster. We both acted as if what we were seeing was real.

That night led me to reflect on how important it is to make our moves in life from the vision that we can see ourselves. Our vision, our dream, our goals - all of it can be seen with so much clarity within our own minds. There will be some people who vibe with the way we describe it, there will be people who cannot envision it at all, either way, neither can fully see what we are seeing until it becomes materially manifested. And even then, some people will continue to perceive what is happening completely differently to the way we do.

When you are immersed in your vision, it will be magical for you. When you explain it to others, sometimes you can muse them into feeling that magic too, a lot of the time they just can't see it. This can feel very deflating, especially to our ego, our mind wants others to understand us. If we let the mind keep driving from this ego desire to be understood we can start to try to convince others to believe us, or worse, take on their doubts as our own. Always remember that they are only responding to you from what they can see, which is not your full vision. So do not let these kinds of people have input into the moves that you are making.

Be ok with looking a little silly to the people on the outside looking in.

When you are creating, when you have a vision for what you want to bring to life in the world, and a vision for the impact you want to make in the world, if this vision is something you deeply care about, you can see the core elements very clearly.

The brain cannot tell the difference between an imagined vision, and your physical vision. If you imagine a situation, your body will respond as if you are in that situation, you can make yourself feel angry and agitated, or sad and crying, with your thoughts and imagined states alone. Looking into a virtual-reality lens, even though part of you knows where you physically are, your brain cannot tell the difference and sends the signals for your body to react accordingly.

When it comes to the visions for your creative endeavours, stay connected to your dreams and make moves from this place of connection. This is part of reprogramming your subconscious mind to accept your vision as reality, in this way you stop subconsciously sabotaging yourself on your way to the material manifestation of your vision.

Your visions are real. And they only need to be real to you.

No one external to you can be as immersed in your vision as you are. No one external to you can interact with your vision in the way that you can.

The doubt of others can trick you into believing that your vision is just made up, and never going to happen, but it is real because it is real to you!

When others are not connected with our vision, and the potential within it, they see the moves we make and think we are crazy, they don't understand why we are doing what we are doing and often it is the people closest to us that will try to talk us into doing something else, they may mean well, but trust that you know better when it comes to your life.

This was certainly the case when I started doing things like buying crystals, oracle cards, doing my life coaching training, and yoga teacher training, all while my professional accounting career was really progressing. It didn't make sense to anyone in my life, but I knew all of those things were important parts of my path. When I left my career after working in the organisation I was in for close to a decade, half a decade of study, tens of thousands of dollars invested, to go and be a yoga teacher and online coach, I had to be really grounded in my belief of my own vision. Many people close to me tried to talk me into making different decisions, but I already knew exactly what I needed to do for me. There are so many points of indoctrination where we are taught to believe other people have greater authority than us when it comes to making decisions about our own life, but I truly believe that there is no greater authority than yourself when it comes to your life. You are the only expert in that area.

It doesn't matter if others don't understand and can never comprehend your actions and the moves you are making. When you are creating something, you are connected to something they just aren't, and maybe never will be. Don't take seriously the advice or the opinions from anyone who is not connected to your vision.

Even when you have 'proven' that you were right, and you created exactly what you said you would, others will look at it and still not see what you do.

Hold the vision you have as sacred. Make moves from what YOU see. Your vision is real because you are connected to it. You give your vision life.

Ideas are like energetic butterflies that love whispering into your ear

I love to visualise ideas as these little energetic butterflies, or light beings that are flying and floating around in the world. These ideas are needed to bring creative things to life. For these ideas to come to life in the world of matter, they need to move through something with primal creative energy, that is, a human being. Your life-force and creative potential draws these little ideas in.

Imagine these little idea butterflies flying around, being drawn to the life-force of certain people and then whispering into their ears, sharing the idea and planting that seed in their mind.

There are billions, maybe even trillions, of these little idea butterflies floating around at any given time and their only objective is to be brought to life. So, they find as many people as possible who may be able to bring them to life. You have many, many ideas being planted in your mind from soft little whispers all throughout each day.

Some ideas are so out there from the way you live your life that you just laugh them off, like the idea of starting a hotdog stand where people on the street can sing karaoke while blindfolded. Some ideas are small and can be immediately manifested, others carry a more long-term visionary quality to them. For some of these ideas, you may tune into their frequency while you are watching a movie and something in it triggers your connection to the idea. Some ideas come to you and you want to fully tune into the belief in your capability of bringing it to life, but your mind ultimately talks you out of it.

All the ideas that could ever be had right now, are floating around. But you are not in an aligned frequency with every idea. They are all there though.

To hear and perceive a certain idea, your creative energy, your life-force, must match its frequency. The idea must be attracted to your energy. As you refine your energy, more refined ideas will be drawn to you.

There are times when we are attracting an idea at an unconscious level, and it will stay with us until we are ready to consciously perceive it. Some of these idea butterflies will plant themselves in your ear and continue whispering until you are ready to hear them, like a constant tickle that you can't seem to shake until you follow it and muse on it. Other ideas that find you may leave for a while in hopes of finding someone else to bring them to life but ultimately come back to you. Some big ideas will draw in all their friends for the ideas you need first in order to put things in place, and then in divine timing you consciously recall the first idea and see the divine synchronicity that was weaving through your life all along.

There are so many ideas already flying around on earth, they are so excited to find someone who can bring them into form in our material world. If they come to you and you ignore them, or you take too long, they will simply fly away and find someone else to bring them to life.

There will be times when you see someone doing something, bringing a creation of their own to life, and you think that you had that idea first and maybe regret that you didn't end up following through and doing what you needed to, to implement it. The person who the idea went to may be someone you know, or a stranger across the globe.

There are also ideas flying around in different dimensions and out in all the corners and space within the cosmos, some of these are only aligned to *your* energy and when you are ready you can channel them through to earth. There will be some ideas that only you have the capacity to bring to life. There will be others that once you have channelled them into our realm and they are here to play, they may fly all around for others to bring to life in their own unique way. Some ideas will be naturally drawn to us, sometimes we need to go and play in the world to find them, sometimes we need to have a certain experience before we are ready for them. There are so many different ways that ideas can come and play with you. This isn't something to overthink about, you are naturally meant to create so this element of creation is innate in that process. When you prioritise your life-force, your creative energy will draw many ideas in.

Some ideas know that they are meant to come into the world at a large scale all at once and they have such a strong impulse to be created, so they will plant the seed in us and immediately go and do the same for many other people. So many people in the world will suddenly have the same idea. Even when this is the case, everyone who chooses to bring the idea to life through them will do it in a unique way. Every expression of the same idea will be different as it comes to life through the creative energy of different people. There will be similarities and maybe recognition that it is part of a wider trend, but it will be different nonetheless.

There are times when trends seem to take over and on the outside it may appear that everyone is copying someone else, but this is rarely the case. There may be times when a large creator has an influence over what others are creating, but even then the 'same' thing is coming into the world in many different flavours.

If we think back to more ancient times, before the internet and before material communication between countries and continents, there are many examples of the same ideas being created and the same ideas being documented. Even though different languages were used and different variations exist, many of the world's religions and spiritual teachings have the same core messaging, that there is a divine Creator. The views of this divine Creator become varied through the interpretation of different humans, yet the essence of the messages coming from this Creator is often very similar. And how ancient pyramids not only exist in Egypt but around the world.

The way we play with ideas has changed since the inception of the internet and more access to information. We can open our laptop or phone and 'Google' 'ideas for….' and many results will come up – but maybe a little idea butterfly came and whispered in your ear to pick up your phone to make that search.

Start to bring your awareness to all the ideas that are dropping in on the daily. Tune into which of these ideas have been very persistent trying to make you hear them, which ideas really turn you on, which ideas it may be time to let go of, before making decisions give yourself the space to play with each of them. How would it look and feel if you were to commit to bringing this idea to life? What would make bringing this idea to life fun and expansive?

This is the process I moved through when I was playing with the idea to create the Spirited Leaders Magazine, an online magazine that I curated and edited for four issues over 12 months. The idea dropped in to start a magazine focused on leadership, spirituality, creation, pleasure, business, and mindset. Initially I thought that it sounded really interesting and like a really cool thing to do BUT my next lot of thoughts were around the practical side of all the elements that would be involved like the layout, planning all the articles, the online hosting parts, and all the other little bits and pieces I wasn't even aware of yet. I took a breath and put those practical elements aside so that I had the space to play with the vision. I promoted myself with the question – what would make this fun? What support would I love to have? What support would I need to have? What elements would I love to create myself? What is the big vision? It was pretty quickly after playing with the vision these prompts stirred up that I was all in to bringing the magazine to life. I allowed myself to get started and the first issue was incredible and it continued to evolve in many ways until it felt complete after one year of creating four issues. In that time I expanded my skills, connections, vision, and self in many ways, and the impact of what was created is still being transmitted in the world.

When you cut yourself off from the potential of ideas at the first sign of doubt or fear, you will likely never bring creation into the world that is a reflection of your potential and creative power. It is simply a mechanism of the mind to ask these what if…? type of questions, you get to shift the questions to be spacious and expansive rather than constricting and depleting.

Even when there is that initial doubt or questions around the 'how' you would actually do something that you have never done before, choose to believe that you are competent enough to work it out as you go, resourceful enough to call in or find what you need, and that there are many different ways you can be supported through your experience.

There are some butterflies that travel to you to give to others and conversely some that go to others to ultimately get to you. There will be times when an idea drops in but you get the sense that someone in your circle would be the perfect person to bring it to life, so you share the idea with them. Ideas are abundant like that.

Sometimes the ideas that you do give birth into the world were designed to be the muse for someone else to feel activated in bringing their own idea to life.

When we trust in the creative flow of energy within the collective we can take a zoomed out view on the purpose each of our ideas has in the world once it has been birthed. Many of your own ideas will lead you into different experiences that needed the first to occur. When you trust in the flow of life your mind loosens its grip on needing any single creation to be 'successful' in any one way.

The expression of your creative energy when you bring ideas to life in the world is how you tune in deeper to your creative energy, which refines what you are attracting and brings you into divine synchronicity where there is ease in flowing along the path.

Your creative energy is so unique and you get to play with and explore all the ideas that are drawn to you, you get to bring life to the ideas that feel exciting and right for you.

Your creations are MAGIC and MEDICINE

If you create something, it will be either magic or medicine for the world.

Read that sentence again. Use it as an affirmation whenever you have the slightest inkling of doubt as to whether your creations are actually meaningful expressions in the world.

Your creations are magic and medicine even if you never see external results. If you don't see anyone else engaging with your creation physically, or buying them, or talking about them, or admiring them, *none* of this takes away from their magic. You do not need external results for your creations to be a work of art that has a meaningful place in the world.

The world around us evolves through every living being on it, the more we evolve personally the more we get turned on and tuned in to our own creative energy, and the more we express through our creative energy, the more we evolve. When we create and express, we contribute to the evolution of the world. Even if the only person you see your creations impacting is yourself.

The joy within yourself from your creative expression is enough. And often the reach of your creations will materially go beyond a personal experience.

Create knowing that your creations, everything that is birthed through your creative energy, is magic and medicine for the world.

There will be times when the things we feel called to create landed within our conscious thought as we channelled through the collective field. We will be willed into creating at times for something that was needed by the collective, this is when your creations become medicine for others, the exact thing they needed to grow, heal, to move forward in their own story of evolution. These creations make far and wide ripples through the world. Through the degrees of separation, the rippled impact can touch every person in some way. This isn't something we need to logically comprehend, or predict, this is a sense to be felt. Feel into your creations carrying a transmission that is needed in the world and that is everlasting as soon as it changes anything. You do not need to see the evidence of impact in order to choose to believe that if you create something, it will be either magic or medicine for the world.

Your creations are magic.

Your creations are magical medicine for the world.

Create for yourself first

Create for yourself, first and foremost, always.

Always create for yourself first. (Just to re-emphasise)

What you do when you create for yourself first, is connect to your creative energy in a pure way. In a way that connects you to pure joy, where the creation process in and of itself *is* the fulfilling part and is what gives you joy.

On the other hand, when we create while holding on to the weight of expectations, pressure, and needing your creations to produce any specific external result, you open leaks in your creative field that can feel very draining and depleting. Your creative expression doesn't deserve the heaviness of this pressure. Nor does it deserve the burden of that responsibility.

Creating to make money, or to get praise, or recognition, or to reward you in any way is ok as an element within your creative process, however when these things become the sole driving force, your creations start to carry the weight of these pressures and expectations. We start to distort the expression and taint the transmission that our creations carry. Beyond that, there is more constriction and force invited in, as opposed to creative flow.

Creating for yourself first invites in lightness.

When you create for yourself first, the creation process in and of itself becomes the rewarding part, the part that fulfils you and satiates your spirit's hunger.

When it comes to creating within your business or in a way that is linked to your source of income – you deserve to thrive and to make money while making things that feel fun and fulfilling to you. When you enter into a creative flow, prosperity is a natural by-product, however it may not always be a logical and direct correlation to a specific creation, or in the exact timeline that you would mentally prefer.

Whenever our creativity is linked to the way we make money, there is likely to be an intertwined relationship between our survival and security, and our creative expression.

An approach that invites in a little more lightness is to begin unravelling your relationship with money with your relationship to our creative expression. You will feel the most liberated in your creative expression when your foundational security and survival needs are met first. This may look like having a part time job to fund your lifestyle and the start up of your business, this may look like living with family, calling in the support available to you, it may be restoring your nervous system and reprogramming your mindset to see that you already have all you need. Do what you need to do in order to feel safe enough to create with joy for yourself as the leading force.

Alchemising the fear of making a mistake and overcoming the inevitable case of imposter syndrome

The fear of making a mistake can be one of the biggest dampers to your creative expression, another is creating only when you are in survival mode which we just began to explore in the previous section.

Last year when I was really getting into drawing and wanted to develop this skill beyond random little scribbles, I decided to do an online drawing class, something that covered foundational basics. In the first class that I did from the first video online that looked interesting, the teacher shared her two rules for her class – first was to only use a blue pencil when sketching, and second was that erasers were forbidden.

Taking her rules seriously, and making the eraser off limits for the duration of her class, was liberating. When I had been drawing previously whether randomly or imitating another image, I would always have the eraser handy and I didn't notice how much it added this little pressure to correct 'mistakes' as soon as they were made and to re-do elements until they were 'perfect,' and all of this created a little bit of hesitation to even begin, thinking that I wanted to get it 'right' the first time and not have to re-do so much!

In this class there was full permission to make mistakes, to keep going, to stay in the process. One exercise was to use the blue pencil to draw circles, on top of each other again and again and to just lightly hold the pencil and keep going, and then to take a step back and to see the perfect circle within the sketch of at least 20, to then use a black pencil to go over to mark the perfect one. If there was pressure from the beginning to use the black pencil to draw the perfect circle in the first attempt, my hold on the pencil would have been much tighter and there is a high likelihood the circle would not have been perfect at all.

The fear of making a mistake often stops you from even beginning. This fear can come from many different places within you, the fear of being rejected as an example, or the fear of not meeting your perfectionist standards that are rooted in the fear of being shamed. Only when you recognise that it is indeed fear that has been pulling the brakes on the creations you want to get started on, can you begin to see the roots of these fears and discern what they are attached to.

All self-proclaimed 'perfectionists' use this title to put a mask on their deep-rooted fear of making mistakes. If you have used this title for yourself, and perhaps even wear it as a badge of honour, I invite a moment of gentle reflection from you. You can hold high standards for yourself, your art, and others, and still be ok with mistakes being a natural part of the creative process.

Allowing mistakes to be part of your creative process is liberating.

Don't let the fear of making mistakes stop you from taking your first step, or drawing your first blue circle. There really are no mistakes, only art on the page which we can then adapt, learn, grow, and evolve from. Tune into this truth in the beginning of your journey.

The most difficulty in your journey will be in the beginning, especially when it concerns something you have never done before, and at times when you feel there are high stakes, getting started in the midst of fear can feel heavy. As Richard Rudd shares in his transmission for the 3rd Gene Key with the shadow of Chaos, "chaos is about beginnings…the greatest challenge in evolution is always at the beginning." When it comes to our creative evolution we can stay in the shadow and only see the chaos, or we can embrace that the beginning is the most difficult part and keep allowing ourselves to move forward. In the story of the 3rd Gene Key this leads you into the Gift of Innovation, where life is designed to "transcend its own initial programming (Difficulty at the Beginning) and discover new and higher forms of consciousness." Richard Rudd shares that "innovation only occurs when you truly begin to think for yourself." To think for yourself you must not think with the fear of the collective, or your own distorted fear. With the Gift of Innovation in the Gene Keys comes optimism and the "dynamic energy at the heart of creation."

When you embrace fear and the fear of making a mistake as part of the process, and something that will only feel heavy at the beginning, you release your grip from the heavy bags, you take the pressure of holding it off your back, and you liberate so much of your creative energy.

Sometimes those high stakes are attached to our inner core wounds around fear of rejection, judgement and so on. When entering into a new creative endeavour whether it be drawing for fun, starting a business, writing a book, anything that you wish to share with others in anyway, there can be this hesitancy of not wanting others to see you while you are learning, not wanting to hear the shit comments like 'you should keep your day job.' There is vulnerability in starting something new, and in sharing your creativity. When you self-source your own acceptance, and seek your joy from the process itself, your attachment to what others may think or say about your art will loosen. Not everyone is going to see the beauty that you do in all of your artful expressions. The people that do connect with your creative expression are going to be in awe of your art. At times that awe will extend to your grace and your willingness to share your art in the way that you do, at times that may be all some people appreciate as opposed to actually liking what you are creating, and this is all ok.

An example for me of people supporting my creative expression and at the same time not loving my art, is my books. When I published my first book, I had so much loving support from people in all areas of my life. I hosted a massive book launch celebration, and many family members and friends bought a signed copy of my book in celebration of me, even though I know they will never read it, at least not in its entirety. This is fine, it is just not content that they resonate with or would enjoy reading. My first book is lovingly displayed in the homes of many of my family members who have never opened it past the first page where I wrote a little note for them. My subsequent books were equally celebrated even when they weren't all purchased by all my loved ones.

My creative process for the way I wrote and published my first book had a massive ripple effect in addition to the ripples of the creation (the book) itself.

This fear of making a mistake, and beyond that the fear of *being seen* making a mistake, or being seen doing something not amazingly the first time you do it, will dilute your creative potential so much.

The creation of my first book was not perfect, there were a small handful of typos in the book, I was a little too excited at the end of the process and just wanted to get it out instead of doing one more final proofread. I had someone hand me a list of said typos after they read the book and even though they did it in the most kind way possible, I did feel the judgement, but I was ok with my book having little imperfections. If I was designing the cover today it would look very different but I worked with what I had and knew at the time and I do love it. There is content within the book that I have evolved beyond that perspective now, but it captures perfectly my views, stories, wisdom, and teaching at the time I wrote it.

To move through your fears of making a mistake in your creative expression –

1. Take on the mindset that – **there is no such thing as mistakes in my creative expression.** There may be little bumps, there may be lessons to learn, I will most likely look back at my art in a year and think 'wow I have improved so much since then, but I still love it exactly as it is.' There are no mistakes that you can't come back from, that you can't learn from, there are no mistakes that are not meant to be part of your creative journey for any particular piece of your art. 'It is impossible for me to make a mistake in my creative expression.' Choose to believe this. Affirm it to yourself.

2. When others point out what they believe to be 'mistakes' in your art – acknowledge this is a 'them' problem and an invitation for them to become more comfortable seeing imperfections in the world. You do not need to take on the feedback and opinion of any one person as truth. Don't take any criticism personally and internalise it. Self-source your own feelings about your art and allow the space for others to have

their own inner feelings and thoughts about your art.

3. Allow the fear to provoke you into excitement, knowing that you are safe to express yourself.

Have fun with your creative expression and remember that everything you create is a work of art in its own right.

Now, let's talk imposter syndrome. This phrase is thrown around a little. Here is the definition according to Google –

Imposter syndrome refers to an external experience of believing you are not as competent as others perceive you to be.

Hand up if you have ever felt like this?

Puts hand up I have. Like when I recorded my first chapter of podcast episodes and felt so lit up by the process, and then an hour later I felt a sudden pit of doubt that made me want to delete the recordings and start again! The doubts coming up were all focused around how I thought others would receive the messages, and how they would perceive me as a result. I thought I needed to be more prepared and make it better.

But after taking a deep breath I grounded in the truth of how amazing those first recordings were. I have listened to those episodes a few times and am impressed with the flow of art within them every time. That first chapter on the podcast formed the basis for Chapter One of this book, and the inspiration behind this entire book.

Sometimes when we do things that are really expansive for us, and often when they involve big emotions like excitement, as soon as our energy lowers from the high just a little we are pulled back down. The mind's attempt to bring us back within our comfort zone. The doubt can spiral into thoughts around us needing to do better before we show anyone our work or our art. This kind of doubt can keep you stuck in the same place indefinitely and even though it feels as if you are doing so much you never really move forward.

Imposter syndrome can paralyse you, or it can act as an invitation into a deeper embodiment of your expansion. Grounding a deeper trust that your art is valuable when it is out in the world.

Often it is self-identified 'perfectionists' who get stuck in imposter syndrome the most. The mind creates an illusion that they need to keep making whatever they are working on 'better.' Of course, you could improve what you are working on, and you can absolutely hold high standards, and choose when you feel it is ready to share. And it is important to bring completion and closure to your creative experiences.

Perfectionism is an expression of fear.

Have an honest look at where you cling to perfectionism and control in your life and creative process, what fear is attached to this?

Your mind will often want to stay in the internal part of the creative process, where it is only you and maybe a select few seeing your art. As soon as it is time to share with a wider audience and time to give others an opportunity to have something to say about what you have created, the fear of rejection, shame, etc. can rear its head and get loud, making you end the creative cycle early and stay in a stagnant loop.

It is important to be able to recognise when you have done enough. To be in reverence for your part in your art.

There is always space for your next piece of art to expand on your current expression.

Remember your creations are magic and medicine, the way you feel drawn to create something holds power – you do not need to adjust for how you believe others will perceive your art.

When you are in your own moments of imposter syndrome -

1.   Take a deep breath, as many as you need to ground back into your body

2.   Remind yourself of what a sneaky little bitch your mind can be and if said bitch is trying to pull you back into a safe space right when you are beautifully expanding with your creation – remind your mind that you are safe in this moment and that you are safe to expand.

3.   Notice when you are trying to keep your creations in, out of fear for others experiencing them in any kind of negative way, or any way that wouldn't meet your mind's expectations. Notice when you are in a loop of starting something, scrapping it, and starting again. In this moment ground your energy by completing something (even if it is just baking a cake).

Expanding on the third point, I have seen this play out with many people. They will have an amazing idea and be so excited by it. For some it is a business idea, they choose a business name, design a logo, do their study, buy their inventory, and at the last-minute right when it becomes the time to actually put something out there to sell, they do a 180 and decide this actually isn't what they want to do and they abandon the entire thing! This can also play out when you buy all the ingredients for this amazing meal you felt an impulse to create and then you end up ordering takeout, use some of the ingredients for other things, and let some of the ingredients rot in the fridge before throwing them out. Then they get a new amazing, totally the one, idea, and the exact same cycle plays out. Nothing ever gets put out into the world or seen through to its creative completion.

You are allowed to change your mind, and this happening in and of itself isn't a bad thing. But if you notice this is a pattern and that you do so much behind the scenes work but never let yourself really put yourself out there to get off the ground – you are very likely getting a hard case of imposter syndrome self-sabotage where you are stuck in a loop of never fully completing anything within its creative cycle.

You can honour your high standards with your willingness to be vulnerable, to be seen. It is not yours to take personally what anyone has to say about what you create.

Polish and refine as much as you like and bring your closure to your creative cycles.

Whenever you suddenly want to pivot in the direction of any kind of creative expression, question where this urge is coming from. Is it being driven by fear? Or is it coming from your creative impulse that something even better for your energy, and your joy could be explored?

When you are creating following the urge of joy your previous work will become the fertiliser for your new art, nothing is ever wasted. When you are in your natural creative cycle everything builds on the last cycle. There will be elements from within your creative expression like your new skills, connections, access, and so many others that you can bring into what you do next. When your work effortlessly builds on the last project it is a sign that you are in the flow of the never ending story of your creative evolution.

If you end the creative cycle early, you likely didn't get to the juice to carry it forward with you and that is why you stay in the repeating pattern until you see it all the way through to get your juice.

It's meant to feel easy

It is meant to feel easy.

It is meant to feel easy.

It is meant to feel easy.

Take a moment to feel into how that statement feels in your body. Does your body accept this truth and feel relaxed by this statement? Or perhaps your body feels a little triggered and rejects the statement.

For the most part, as a collective society, we have been conditioned to believe that everything worth doing needs to be hard work, and to think that the people who 'work hard' are the most honourable, dedicated, even saintly, of us all and thus are the most deserving of all the rewards life may produce. Work has become synonymous with 'hard work.'

What happens when we do not embrace that life and our creative expression can feel easy, our sneaky little mind comes in to make it unnecessarily harder in an attempt to convince ourselves that we are working hard and therefore we really are deserving. Your mind and your nervous system is so used to a certain level of stress that it drives your subconscious to keep you at this point for that dopamine hit of worthiness.

There are many ways the things we do can be challenging, and challenge is what helps us grow and evolve. When you bring awareness to what is unnecessarily hard, you will see it is likely an attachment to doing unimportant things and the ego attaching importance to those tasks.

Everything that is a skill is buildable. We can learn how to do anything. Some skills we pick up very quickly, some take a while to build our proficiency. Some skills we will never reach the level of the people we compare ourselves to. Some skills we are objectively 'bad' at but we still love doing it. We can build our skill in any area. How we build our skills is through practice. Often it is not practice alone which helps us build our skills, whenever I hear the saying 'practice makes perfect' I am taken back to my gymnastic lessons from when I was in primary school, my coach would always say 'practice doesn't make perfect, perfect practice makes perfect.' That is to say that what you are practising is what you are perfecting and you could unwittingly be perfecting how to do something 'wrong.' It is possible to be self-taught in many areas but there is still likely a reference point and something external you are using for confirmation that you are on the right track.

When it comes to your creative expression, there isn't necessarily a 'wrong' way. But there are ways that allow the process to be full of much more ease and joy.

If anything within your creative expression feels hard right now, here is what I recommend you look into –

1.   Embrace the fear and chaos in the beginning. Let the fear expand you rather than constrict you.

2.   Think back to your childhood, what came naturally to you? This could be any type of skill, it could be how you connected with others and made friends, it could be the way you told stories, or the way you organised your bedroom, or literally anything else.

Do these things still feel easy and natural to you?

If it does – amazing!

If it doesn't – maybe this natural love felt like it was slapped out of you, or at one point it was too child-ish. Take time now to return to these things that felt easy, natural, and fun for you as a child.

Transition back into your natural gifts and talents, with your evolved awareness.

3. When you are exploring something that you are not naturally talented at, remind yourself that you can build any skill. Drop the pressure and expectation that you need to be 'good' at everything straight away (or at all).

4. Re-examine what past authority figures have told you about your creativity, or any skill. Is it actually your primary school teacher's voice telling you that you are not 'good at art.' Or 'maths' or anything else. So your mind is telling you now that in order to do anything involving those things will be so hard. But maybe if you let the voice of others go within yourself, you would realise how capable you are at learning something new, or that you are already doing it well.

5. Let things be messy and magical at the same time – see the magic within the mess, and the mess within the magic.

Writing used to feel really hard for me. But when I think back to when I was a child, so much of my creative expression flowed into different forms of writing. When I was younger I loved writing in journals, whether it was detailing what happened in a day, expressing feelings, or making up stories. I had so many childhood journals, but then when my three younger sisters got a bit older and made a habit of finding them, reading them aloud to the family, or telling other people what I wrote, no matter how many locks or different hiding places I used, I stopped writing in journals. I only returned to journal writing again as an adult rediscovering self-love. I also loved writing songs, these were just for fun. I remember when we would go to family friend's houses and all my siblings would be running around with the other kids I would be sitting down with paper and pencils, writing songs. I don't think they were any good, but I also gave up this hobby when I was told I wasn't a good singer (a story in my first book).

The longer I was in school the more I realised how academically inclined I was in maths, and how I wasn't at as high a level in my English subjects. Over time, I gave less of my focus and energy to the subjects I thought I wasn't that good at. I remember in Year 9 and 10 my English teachers made comments around my 'poor' grammar and writing. By this time I just thought that I was 'bad' at English. Whatever that means. Then I went into Year 11, a new school, and a new teacher. That year I got straight A's in English and was ranked second in my class. (I was top of my class for Maths, Accounting, and Business). This started to turn my views around on my writing. I noticed that the grading was far less skewed towards my spelling and gave much more weight to my ideas, the way I structured my thoughts, and communicated my position.

I may not be a 'good' writer to the standards or opinions of some, but I love the way I channel, and communicate through my writing. It is part of my art. When I put the pressure and expectations down around what I think others would want my writing to look like, it flows through easily.

In different environments, with different mentors, and different goals, you will experience different results. There are many times when your low grades are your teacher's failing, not yours. Now as an adult, don't continue giving their criticism a voice in your head. It does not matter what your grades were in school, or the commentary around those grades.

I was working with a client who told me she was an 'average person', let's call her Jessica. When I asked Jessica what evidence she had for this wild (completely untrue) statement she was making about herself, the only reasoning she had was that she got B's in school and her friends got A's and that is just how she is in life (mind you we were talking years and years past her school days). I called BS on this story instantly and called Jesscia into a moment of reflection. You are not being graded by life. And even if your mind has made up some metric to determine the value of people in the world (how much money they make, how much they weigh, where they live etc.) that is just another BS measure when it comes to determining a human being's intrinsic value.

Once this story Jessica had in her mind for many years was brought into the light to see clearly, she could see the plot holes in the conclusions she had drawn about herself and her place in life. Letting this story go opened up so much ease in Jessica's creative expression and she was able to pour that into writing her first book that she had started but felt stuck in.

The beautiful thing about creativity, and creation, is that we all have our own differentiated flavour that we get to express into the world. There is no rubric cube grading, or judge that can determine any one creation better than any other.

Your art is subjective. You disliking another person's art does not make their art less beautiful. The same goes for your art with the subjective views of others.

Even those who you once looked up to, or still do, have subjective and biased opinions. Not allowing these to interfere with your creative process, or your relationship with your art is a big piece in allowing your creative expression to flow through you and from you in a way that feels easy.

There may be moments when you forget how wonderfully creative you are, or how sacred and beautiful every single piece of your art is, and that is ok.

When you subconsciously punish or sabotage yourself because your mind needs things to feel harder to convince itself you are deserving of the results, this is ok.

Whatever creative path you take, embrace these little bumps as invitations for a deeper belief and embodiment in your creative power. When you are anchored to your natural rhythm (which we will explore more in Chapter Three), these little bumps are only obstacles that you can easily and playfully manoeuvre because you have everything you need for your wild adventure.

You can allow your creative expression to emerge easily, while thriving in the life you get to live.

In your creative journey your action can be full of ease, each step being effortless but not without effort.

A final note here – you have nothing to prove to anyone and you never need to defend yourself. You do not need to manage those that may feel uncomfortable at the thought of your life and creative expression flowing easily.

Your creative impulse: summary

- Your creative energy is innately part of your being, it is one in the same with the energetic current that gives you life. You are creative because you exist.

- The gentle path to allowing your unique creative style to emerge, is to play in the process of imitation, innovation, to invention.

- You see your creative vision more vibrantly and fully than anyone else ever could, thus is it important for you to make moves from what you see rather than taking advice from others who are not capable of seeing your vision.

- Creative ideas are energetic beings, they are little flirts that are so attracted to you and love whispering into your ear in the hopes you will bring them to life. Ideas are everywhere and always available to you.

- If you feel called to create something, it is needed in the world.

- The creative process *is* the fulfilling part.

- Fear and mistakes are part of the creative process, you are too powerful to allow them to keep holding you back from sharing your art with the world.

- It is meant to feel easy, because when you are in flow with your creativity you are in flow with life itself.

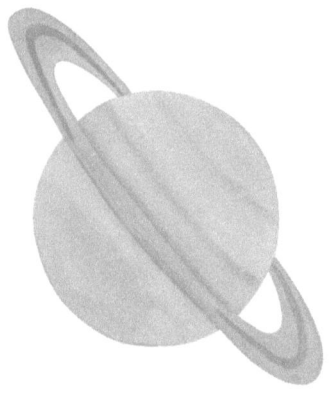

CHAPTER TWO
THE WORLD AS YOUR MUSE

The world is an exciting place, so much to see, touch, and taste. Place the rose-coloured lens over your eyes, to see all the magic previously in disguise.

Sacred Symbolism – Saturn

Saturn, known as the planet of karma, takes around 29 Earth years to move around the Sun. Even though its years are long, its days are short lasting only ten hours and fourteen minutes. This is a poetic metaphor for how we humans live: the years feel so long when we are in them, but the days go by so quickly when we aren't fully awake to the life we are living, when we aren't seeing the beauty of the world and extending the present moment by taking it in. When the days go by quickly, all of a sudden, the years do too.

This planet symbolises structure, ambition, and periodic renewal. It teaches you the lessons of life, directing you into the action needed to learn those lessons. The day Saturday was named after Saturn, a day we typically allow for all activities - work, play, and some rest. Usually, it is on Saturday that errands are run, we actively go out and do things in the world, we plan parties and dinners for this day, and then we start to wind down preparing for our day of rest.

Your Saturn Return begins when this planet returns to its position in space at the time you were born. This usually takes place when you are between 27-30 years old. It is an astrological coming of age, the marking of time to start becoming aware of the lessons life has been teaching you. The return usually accompanies a big change. In order to be schooled by life, you must live your life! You must be out in the world and soaking it in. This first year of Saturn in your life is about taking risks, living fully, making mistakes, and getting to know the world around you. And then life will test you, in an expansive way that will lead your next big move after reminding you all you have experienced and learnt.

Your second Saturn Return happens in your mid to late 50s, and your third in your mid to late 80s. Each time marks a new chapter, when you allow the world around you to be your place of higher learning.

There are times when Saturn will prompt you back, when there is something you aren't moving forward with on your own. This is when Saturn goes into retrograde, dipping back into the previous sign, then forward again, helping you move forward too.

The gentle approach to romanticising life

The world becomes your greatest muse when you allow yourself to widen your view and begin seeing all of what is around you. When we narrow our view, we lose sight of so much magic that could be the catalyst to a new creation or to us fully living in that moment. Romanticising your life begins to widen your view and shifts your mindset and perspective to see the beauty in all around you.

This romanticisation of your life can co-exist with realism, you don't get lost in the clouds, (although it is fun to play there at times) this is about opening your eyes and seeing each element present as an important and beautiful part of your unfolding story.

Take a moment to put on some (metaphorical) rose coloured glasses. These will help you widen your view and to become open to more of the beauty that is already around you.

How would you see your life?

What dullness would suddenly fill with colour?

How would you move through your day differently if you saw everything around you as something truly magical?

We are living on a spinning rock that rotates around a ball of fire, floating in space. Our bodies are made up of the particles of stardust. Sounds pretty magical to me. So it isn't too far a stretch to believe that there is magic happening all around you and that everything is in fact some kind of magic.

In the monotony of how adult life can easily become, at times it takes some prompting for us to remember and take notice of the magical elements all around us. To be reminded of the magic that is innately infused with every aspect of our lives, we need look no further than nature. Get out of your house, or your air-conditioned office, and go and be out in the world.

Notice the spiral on a snail's back, notice how that same exact spiral appears many times in nature. Notice the cocoons hanging that will soon open for a butterfly that was once a caterpillar, take notice of all the trees you see and recognise just how long they have been so tall and mighty and how they were once a tiny little seed. Notice the wind in your hair, the dirt in your fingernails, and all the little elements you would usually ignore and just pass by.

Romanticising your life is about recognising the magic that is already there.

It is not about ignoring or justifying dangerous, abusive, or internally destructive situations. When you look at these with your rose-coloured glasses, maybe the magic you see will be your capacity to make some kind of change. Or perhaps it is not safe for you in this moment to romanticise this aspect of your life yet, and this is ok.

To romanticise your life, you need to be present in your life.

Where are you distracted by the grey clouds in your inner world – where is your mind taking you out of the present moment?

You do not need a solid answer for all these questions I have dropped in, let them sit at the back of your mind to contemplate. Muse on these prompts.

While romanticising life, there is so much space to day-dream and tune into the energy of what could be. These daydreams can lead you into action, or it can be a moment of fun to imagine.

When in your daydreams, it can be tempting to get stuck in the fantasy, where you see something you want but never take any action. If you are attached to the fantasy it can be depleting for your energy. When it comes to your daydreams that are fuelled by a desire you want to see manifested in the material world, know you have the power to ground the vision and start moving forward. This is a story told within the archetype of the 41st Gene Key.

Living in the shadow of Fantasy of the 41st Gene Key is like living in your mind, where you mentally experience how to live your dream, you are holding all the ingredients there, but you never come out of your mind to see that you already have what you need in the material world to make the dream a reality.

Richard Rudd shares that "it is because of this 41st Shadow that our planet is populated by people who dream of a better life but who, for one reason or another, are unable to bring these dreams into reality." The primary reason for this is that when you spend too long in the daydream or the fantasy without being grounded you "become addicted to the hope that the dream brings to your mind, rather than actually launching off in the direction of the dream."

When you make it a practice of romanticising your life you begin to see that the 'hope' that what you want to create and how you want to live is available to you, it isn't something you need to reserve for your inner fantasies, the hope and the magic exist in the world you are living in. Your fantasy daydreams can be a beautiful and thrilling place to play in, but if you stay there too long without any grounding or action in our material world these fantasies can become an escape to living your romantic life.

The light within this shadow of fantasy, is the gift of anticipation. A beautiful gift that attunes you to the unfolding storylines all around you. The shift between being lost in fantasy and into the gift of anticipation is by grounding your fantasies, believing that they can be materialised. Maybe not in the exact way you envision in your mind, but the seed of the desire is available to you. When you start playing with your fantasies through your life, in the world, you will see all the beautiful elements around you that are a part of the unfolding story you are anticipating.

Play in the world like it is a great romance, like every element within it is part of the story, widen your view to see it all. Think poetically about what you see, allow all of your senses to be involved in every moment. What feels like a romanticisation of life for you will be unique and special for you.

Contemplation – a portal to revelation

The Art of Contemplation is a core teaching within The Gene Keys. There is a book by that title written by Richard Rudd and it is interwoven into all materials within the framework.

I first learnt about The Art of Contemplation in my first deep dive into The Gene Keys. Richard Rudd explains that there are three classic paths to truth: meditation, concentration, and contemplation. Contemplation being the path used within the gene keys voyage. This core teaching within the entire gene keys framework underpins how our inner wisdom becomes activated through our work with the transmission.

Meditation is the passive path where you observe what is, concentration is the active path of effort to change what is. Contemplation gets the best of both worlds, being in the middle of the spectrum and having elements from each.

In the path of contemplation your daily life becomes your greatest muse. You simply have an object or focus for your contemplation and you muse on it at the back of our mind as you live your life. There is no need for pressure or force, the revelations will simply drop in as you are out in the world.

I unknowingly used to practise this all the time whenever I was learning something new and particularly when I was in school working on assignments. I made a habit of reading the questions, topics, and tasks involved and then putting it down to begin much closer to the due date. There would be many instances when I felt like I had no idea what I would write when I did my first read over the assignment, but all I needed to do was allow my mind to become aware of it, and many ideas and thoughts would begin percolating, insights would drop in as I was out in the world doing other things, and I would see the dots joining together in my classes and thoughts. When it was time to sit down and write, the floodgates were open and the pages filled. I noticed a harsh difference when I left that first read through to the last minute.

I have been through a similar process in writing this book, although in a very conscious way. Many of my other books came to life very quickly. I wrote and published my first book in just six weeks and one of my poetry books in just three weeks. This book on the other hand called for spaciousness and deep contemplation. After I became clear on the topics and core message of this book, with a draft layout for each chapter, this book called for me to be out in the world, to see the dots joining in the interconnected web of creation, to see how my favourite pop culture references, spiritual insights, and personal stories were all part of the same story. This book called for me to fully live in the world while my mind and awareness took in and moulded all it needed for this book to come to life in the most potent and poetic way.

I am a natural deep thinker, and there are times I get lost in my thoughts and fall down an anxious spiral. But now I practise contemplation by using something for my thoughts to ponder on. The notes section in my phone is full of spontaneous downloads of insight and revelation, some used in my creations, and some just expressed in that moment.

The biggest shift that has occurred for me since practising gentle contemplation was in the realisation that there is never anything that I *need* to do. My body knows what to do, and how to lead me into the 'right' decisions. I simply get to allow the revelations to drop in, and allow my creative impulse to guide me in what art I make, while I live life. This realisation felt like a breath of fresh air. If you have read my first book, you will know how much pressure I grew up with and that pressure grew into heaviness. Contemplation engenders lightness, while still moving you forward as an active participant in your story.

You aren't a passive observer as you are in the path of meditation, and you aren't a forceful pusher like you are in the path of concentration. There is certainly a time and place for both of these paths for certain people. You get to choose how you live. In my perspective, the path of contemplation is the most conducive to living your creative life as the work of art is and was always meant to be.

Alchemise intimidation into inspiration

There is inspiration everywhere in the world, especially in the lives, moves, and actions of other people. Sometimes on the surface of that inspiration is a whole lot of intimidation that we need to cut through to the core of.

Take a moment to ponder the last time you felt insanely intimidated in the presence of someone else, or in the presence of their art. What about that experience made you feel intimidated?

One moment for me was in 2021 when I went to my first pole dancing class, I kept seeing videos and thought it would be fun to try. The class I went to was dance based where we learnt the choreography to a new dance that involved the pole. In the first class I went to, I was the only new person there, and the only one with my body type. Everyone else there was in either very short shorts or just their underwear, some wearing the very high pole dancing heels, and all very experienced. I was wearing full length leggings, a T-shirt, and they gave me spare knee pads that barely fit me. There was a big mirror across the whole front wall which made me feel even more on display and not fitting into the picture of all who were there. They all effortlessly could lift themselves up and do all the pole moves (it is much harder than the pros make it look!). When it came to the dance choreography, I was in awe at how effortlessly they picked it up and how amazing they looked doing it. With the big mirrors around the room, I felt like I could see the stark difference between us even more. I felt very intimidated at the beginning of the class and for some moments throughout, but I made the decision that I would choose to feel inspired rather than intimated. To admire their artful expression with their bodies and to accept that I would not look like that in my first ever attempt, but how inspiring to imagine. When I let go of the thoughts of not being as good as the others around me, and stopped focusing on the mirror, I started to feel the moves in my body and have fun during the class!

It can be tempting to see people who have mastered their craft, or are just naturally talented, or have been practising for a while, and to feel the intimidation sink in. When you allow yourself to feel it fully and accept yourself in the moment you are in, you transcend this feeling in your body and allow it the space to become inspiration.

After that first class I took some private lessons where a personalised choreographed dance was taught to me in a pace I could keep up with (these were very fun) and I also took classes that covered the foundations. The journey felt fun to explore.

When you first immerse yourself into a field you are going to see the art of people who have been playing there for much longer than you. Some had much more resources and access than you while they grew up and were able to pursue this their entire lives. Some were just born with natural talent. Some have very talented mentors who opened doors. Some have practised for many, many hours to hone their craft. At first glance your mind can convince you that they arrived at the same time as you and they are just better and you will never be good enough so you should just go home. But every skill is buildable (go back to Chapter One if you need this reminder again).

AND not all of our craft needs to be something that we excel at. We can be inspired to just have fun! Those pole dancing classes I was taking never had any pressure applied to lead me anywhere. You do not need to monetise or be recognised for every artful experience you have or for all of your creative expressions.

You do not need to be good at everything, your art doesn't need to be good. Be inspired to simply create, to fully live, to try something new – this inspiration could lead you into an amazing moment, or it may unfold in many unexpected ways. It doesn't matter. Let yourself be inspired! This applies to your personal hobbies, your business or work, your relationships, and all you do in life.

Infusing artfulness into the mundane

The way you do the dishes can be infused with your creative energy to make it a work of art. The way you conduct a difficult conversation, the way you apply your makeup, the way you decorate your home, the way you hang your laundry, and even the way you put on your socks – all of this can be an artful expression of your creative life-force.

The 'mundane' tasks of we adults usually consist of any kind of housework, cooking, cleaning, getting dressed, making the bed, driving around, running errands, all those things that are repetitive and involve the maintenance of our existence. Because they become so repetitive over the years we can create this narrative that we can only do them when distracted, when there is nothing better to do, when we are procrastinating, or we just have to force ourselves through them. It may not be like this for every task, but there are likely some that feel like they are always lurking around the corner needing to be done again (for me it is hanging laundry and getting petrol for my car).

All of these mundane tasks are not going anywhere (some can be outsourced or delegated but we are focusing on the ones that you currently are responsible for doing here) and you get to infuse as much of your artful and creative expression into performing these tasks as you do in all other areas of your life that you think are more fun.

Choose one task that needs to be done today and play with how you could make it the most fun, or how you could add just a pinch of joyful art into the moment you are doing it.

When you begin to allow these mundane tasks to be artful two things usually happen.

One, you stop dreading or avoiding them and save yourself a lot of mental energy. They take up much less space in your life when you aren't constantly thinking about needing to do them.

Two, you cultivate presence. Presence that you can bring into any moment which is a conduit for your natural and effortless creative expression. This brings your creative juices into much more of your life.

Earlier today, at the time of writing, I was at my sister's house and she got out a little plaster statue for me and my two year old nephew to paint together. We painted Woody and Buzz in a very colourful way and then our painting moved to a piece of paper, we moved from brushes to painting with our fingers and then our whole hands. My little nephew teaches me a lot about being present and having fun, in this instance every time his hands, which were covered in paint, touched the paper he made a sound effect followed by a laugh. By the end of this he was covered in paint, all over his hands, somehow all over his feet too, and of course covering his clothes. The mess was a work of art. Will the art we created in that moment end up in a museum? No, it will be lucky to not be in the bin by the end of the week. But, the energy of that art will live on in my memories, and in both of our hearts. I know this sounds a little more exciting than the average mundane moment of life, but this is the energy that my nephew brings into every moment. And that most kids do effortlessly. We have so much to learn from kids when we allow our life lessons to come from all of life.

A cardboard box can become a spaceship, covering your eyes with your hands can become the funniest game in the world, a tree can become a new friend, and eating food can be a whole-body experience that takes you to a new dimension.

Hanging your laundry on the clothesline can become your space to dance and intuitively move your body.

Shopping for your groceries can become the time where you have a soulful conversation with an errand buddy.

Cooking can become a time to experiment and play with different flavour combinations.

Washing the dishes can become a practice of presence in and of itself, sensually experiencing every sensation.

Going to the gym can be a practice of deeply tuning into your body and how it feels within every movement.

Having a shower and exfoliating your body can be accompanied with a visualisation that you are energetically scrubbing off all that doesn't serve you in life.

Going for a walk can have a random cartwheel, or some skipping included.

Start with what feels like a dreadful chore and play with the idea of making it a work of art.

There is no pressure for every single moment to be high energy and fun, there is no pressure to ignore when you are feeling frustrated that there is so much to do especially if you don't have a lot of support available right now to do it, but there is nothing to lose making the things you are already doing feel more playful and artful.

In your artful presence for these typically mundane moments, the most random parts or thoughts can become big musing points that lead to some of your most creative work. And the moment of artful joy is enough of a reason for this practice in and of itself.

The power of contrast and staying in motion

Even when you are infusing art into your daily experiences, and your imagination fuels new inner experiences, living in the exact same way everyday can become monotonous.

Inviting contrast into your life opens you to new energy, different perspectives, and more beauty within the world. Your creativity thrives when offered contrasting experiences. This contrast engenders more creativity and greater clarity.

Inviting contrast into your life is as simple as moving into different places and environments and immersing in them to any degree.

Contrast in your life can look like travelling to new places in the world, going to different places to meet new people, going to different events, all things that give a contrast to your daily life opens the space for new ideas and the clarity to see the solutions to the challenges you are facing in your daily life.

Something as simple as driving a different route to the one you usually take every day, or choosing a different path every time you go for a walk. Going to a different café than your regular, even ordering something different from your go-to choice. Reading a book or watching a movie in a different genre to what you would usually choose. There are so many subtle ways to invite contrasting experiences into your life.

Go out and be in the world while you immerse in different experiences, places, cultures, and all else.

Travelling is an exciting way to offer contrast in our life, living in the world outside of our homes that we spend so much time in. Some of my best ideas have dropped in while I was travelling. Like when I was living in New Zealand and heard someone mention they were a life coach and was immediately inspired to explore what that meant which led me to sign up to complete a life coaching certificate. Or when I went on a pilgrimage hike in Japan and was inspired to do my yoga teacher training. Or when I was staying at my cousin's house in Melbourne for a week and poems were rapidly flowing through me into a book that I published shortly after getting back home. And so many little ideas for offers, projects, and personal interests that came out of my many weekend and other overseas trips.

Allowing yourself to see what others are doing and how they are doing it can open space for many ideas to spark. Also being in the energy of other cultures, environments, and situations we wouldn't usually get to be a part of allows us to be around many more ideas and for our creativity to be all juiced up. This isn't at all about taking ideas from others or culturally appropriating anything, this is all about what is a turn on for your creative energy and how the whole world becomes your muse the more you explore and play in it.

When life becomes too repetitive our mind learns how to slip us into autopilot during our repetitive activities. Have you ever got in your car to drive home, without thinking you put your seatbelt on, foot on the brake, start the ignition, and suddenly you arrived without any active memory of your drive. Or you get on your phone and suddenly hours have passed? That is what autopilot looks like. It speeds you through time with no memory of presence. Going into autopilot leaves no space to be creative.

Choosing to drive a different way home, or cooking something different for breakfast, or anything that takes you out of an ingrained routine, forces you to be present and focused in the moment, when you add a relaxed state of presence to this, it is a prime time for creative thoughts to gently drop in. When I am on long distance drives I am constantly channelling and musing on different ideas in between singing along to music.

What areas of your life are calling for contrast?

What adventure do you feel called to embark on?

When you think you will do these things later it becomes easy to slip into autopilot, weeks, months, years, or even decades can pass before you realise how long it has been that you allowed space for your creative energy to simply play in the world through the way you live your life. Make a conscious choice now to live a life full of experiences that contrast your daily life.

New ideas will always come. When you stay in motion you attract more motion and build the momentum in the way you experience your creative energy and the way your creative ideas come to life.

Constant stopping and starting can stagnate your creative energy and make it harder to keep starting again. Rather than sprints and long sleeps, pick up a more relaxed consistent pace that has the space for occasional sprints and pauses.

Staying in motion with your creative living and creative expression becomes easier once you have started, and by having prompts within your daily life to remind you. This can be a weekly check-in with yourself, an alarm on your phone, a sticky-note on your mirror, whatever it is, make it so it cannot fall into background noise that you can avoid. In the next chapter we will explore more around the tempo most aligned for your creative motion.

In a world you could create anything, how to choose what ideas you follow

You are always creating something, and new ideas are always coming in. Begin to bring more awareness to what you are creating and how you are deciding what to create.

Going back to lessons in Chapter One, remember that ideas are little flirtatious things that want your attention. They want you to choose them. These idea butterflies are abundant in nature and are not in competition with each other, they are so ethereal that they do not have an awareness of our human limitations. For all they know you have the power to bring every idea in the world to life. So don't get annoyed and impatient at all the ideas that are drawn to you, they have the purest intentions.

Before you act on ideas that arrive in your field, pause for a moment to play. Play with the idea, play with many ideas, and then you will be in a place to commit your creative energy.

You play with ideas by hearing their whispers, allowing the sense of possibility to excite you, visualising what the creative cycle of each idea could play out as and how you would flow through it.

After the play is done, you can begin to filter through your ideas in a way that aligns with your creative energy and creative expression.

This is where you can bring awareness to what filter you are using to sort these creative ideas. If the filter in your mind has become clogged up and dirty with doubts and other limiting thoughts, it is time to clean those up so that the filter you are using is actually serving you and the ideas that you have just played with.

Make a list of all the usual doubts that arise when you think of pursuing something new, or creating something that you feel drawn to. Some common offenders are 'not enough time,' 'not smart enough,' 'someone has probably already done it,' 'no one will like it anyway.' What are the specific doubts clogging up your creative filter? List them in detail, and then visualise yourself inside your mind cleaning them out of the filter and placing them where they belong. Some may be complete trash and in the rubbish bin they go, some may be compost for the beautiful garden in your mind, some may be the provoker to better beliefs, and some may be fear in disguise that gets put in the back seat. Use whatever analogy or metaphor you like to represent the landscape of your mind.

Once this creative filter has been cleaned up a bit, you can start to look at the functioning of this filter and how it is working.

I see my mental filter to be a multi-dimensional-multi-phase sorting machine, all ideas are filtered through a series of prompts that ultimately determine which basket they end up in.

The prompts may vary depending on the elements of a specific idea, but these are generally what I will use.

1. Does my vision for this idea feel fun? Is my role in this vision something I would love to be a part of?

2. Does this creative idea, and the way I would bring it to life, align with my vision for the world, the person I am, my values, and my ideals?

3. What would need to be put into place for me to bring this idea to life? What resources, time, support, etc. are needed? Do I currently have access to what I need? Or, am I willing to work out a way to get what I need?

4.   What is the life cycle of this creative idea? Would I be committed to see it all the way through? (or might I get bored at some point? If so, would that be ok with me?)

5.   Would bringing this idea to life now interfere with my priority commitments? (Could I move things around if needed? Do I have space coming up?)

Sometimes these prompts lead to more questions and I follow the thread until I arrive at a decision, usually the idea falls into one of these four categories

1.   This is an amazing idea, but it is not for me, I lovingly let it go back out into the ether.

2.   I love this idea but do not have the space right now, I will keep it in my possible idea notes to maybe come back to.

3.   I am not the right person for this idea, but I am going to share it with these people who I think will be the most amazing fit in bringing it to life.

4.   Yes, I am all in, let's go!!!!

Bringing awareness to the filter in your mind that ideas are constantly moving through can help to settle the overwhelm of too many ideas, which is very common when you start to creatively revive your life-force energy.

What you allow within your filter can also help to keep you grounded from all of your abundant play in the world of infinite possibilities. You really could do an infinite amount of things, in an infinite amount of ways, your imagination and creative attraction has no bounds or limits, but your human-ness does have limits and you can't bring to life every single idea that you have had dropped into your awareness.

Your filter is your beautiful inner tool to ensure the creative ideas you do follow through with are the most potent, juicy, and perfect for you.

Creating your own signs from the universe

Maybe you asking for a sign, is the sign?

There are many spiritual teachers who will share advice around asking the universe for a sign. Whether that is a blue butterfly, four leaf clover, or red car, the sign is meant to act as confirmation that you are on the right path. I have set the intention to receive many signs over the years and this is something that can be fun to play with. In the energy of this being fun it feels like you are flirting with the universe and in its cosmic nature it uses the world to provide that sign to you.

But what happens when we overly rely on these external signs as confirmation that we are on the 'right path' is that we start to dilute the trust we have in our own intuition and the inner signs within our body that are always communicating with us. And this makes us always look outward for answers, desperately clinging and reaching for the answer we want coming from anywhere outside of us.

In Taylor Swift's song Death By A Thousand Cuts she speaks of asking the traffic lights if everything is going to be alright. Those traffic lights respond with not knowing, an externalisation of her not knowing the answer and being desperate enough to ask anything to give her a sign. In her song Cornelia Street, from the same Lover album, she speaks again of lights giving her a sign, but this time she states that they pointed her in the direction she was already going. That is the sign she wanted so that is what she made the lights mean in that moment.

Often this is what happens when we ask for signs out in the

world, we give what we see the meaning that we want it to have.

Another example is in the movie The Little Rascals. Alfalfa is sitting up in a treehouse-like structure with a flower, picking each petal 'she loves me,' 'she loves me not.' Until he gets to the last petal and excitedly exclaims 'she loves me!' With full confidence in that statement as the universe confirmed it through a flower. The scene then pans out to reveal the ground with a large pile of flower petals and stems, revealing all the flowers that did not land on 'she loves me' to give him the sign he wanted. He was looking for an outside sign, but only one that would confirm what he wanted to see.

So what if we used our seeking of a sign as confirmation of a sign from the beginning, rather than first convincing ourselves that a sign needs to come from somewhere else?

What if you looking for the sign out in the world, was the sign to look inwards for your answers?

But also, what if everything in the world around you was already a sign? What if you could apply whatever meaning you wanted to whatever you saw in the world? – Well, you can.

There are of course things that we could take as signs (and red flags) all around us – but the thing is that none of them really matter because they only ever have the meaning that we give to them.

It can be really fun and flirty to play with the universe by asking for signs and applying meaning to the things we see and experience, but it stops being fun and playful when it starts stalling your life or leading you to doubt your own wisdom or decisions.

While you play with the 'signs' you see out in the world keep looking within, see that these external signs are reflected from your inner knowing. You create your own signs.

Your life is full of Easter Eggs, messages hidden in plain sight that symbol something from your past or hint at something to come. Like all the best Easter Eggs that Taylor Swift includes in everything she does, they become obvious once what they were hinting to has been revealed. Until then you can have fun playing with what may contain the hidden messages and what they may mean, and it stays playful as long as you don't attach to any theory too seriously. The MCU is also masterful at dropping in Easter Eggs, but even here they are just a fun bonus, maybe even a joke, they are not to distract from the main storyline of the hero we are following in the part of their story they are currently in, the same is true for you.

You do not need to decipher all these Easter Eggs within your life, you do not even need to see them all the time. But know they are there and they will become obvious as your story evolves.

Your story is evolving internally and being reflected into the world, all signs and all these little hints at what is to come are being reflected through your inner world.

When you play with this in your creative life it has to dawn on you that you cannot make a 'wrong' decision. There will always be a sign out there to encourage you to go ahead and do what you want to do, but before you even see the sign your inner knowing has already declared it so, you create all the signs you see. Reclaim this beautiful power.

See the art above, below, and within

In your practice of presence your eyes will be open to all the hidden beauty above, below, and within. Look up to the clouds and you will see moving images of all kinds of animals, and many other objects. Most times they are not obvious until you allow your gaze to look through the shape you expect a cloud to be.

Look at a snail and see the spiral of the universe on its shell. What else do you see?

Look at the tree where the natural openings look resemblant to a vulva or some other beautiful body part. Notice how the tree branches remind you of human lungs.

When you look beyond what is there, you see the beauty within. Just like Michelangelo, the Italian sculptor and artist (not the ninja turtle), famously said "every block of stone has a statue inside it and it is the task of the sculptor to discover it. I saw the angel in the marble and carved until I set him free."

In your creative endeavours look around in the world and see within what your eyes can see. Take in the beauty of the world and then pierce through it.

There was once the first person in the world to use a tree to make paper, or a chair, or even a house. It is amazing to think back to how all the elements in nature were first used to create something else. With respect to nature, and no pressure for your creation to be completely original, what do you see or sense that is calling you to make art out of it?

The world is your muse, go out and gaze into what you see until you see the art within it.

Wouldn't it be great if…?

I first heard this question from Marie Forelo in one of her MarieTV videos when she spoke about her team meetings. Marie explained that her team would go around in a circle for everyone to fill in the blank to this question and put forward whatever flowed with the prompt. Some ideas presented were very out there and were just fun to discuss in the moment, others couldn't be implemented but inspired a wider discussion, and then there were those ideas that felt like they came out of nowhere and at the same time they couldn't believe noone thought of it sooner, and they were able to be put in place, those ideas that would not have been spoken and implemented without the space to be prompted in this way.

We all have access to different ideas, all those energetic butterflies that hang around us, our capacity to connect these ideas into the wiring of our brain, in order to communicate these ideas to others, will build with how we become prompted.

Prompting can come from the outside world, like when we use the world as our muse, and we can also form a habit of prompting ourselves to think in more open and creative ways to consistently enter an inspired state of mind.

I am constantly using the 'wouldn't it be great if…?' prompt. When something isn't going smoothly this question comes to my mind while thinking of the things it would be cool to have or to work in a certain way to make it more efficient, effective, or fun. Often a quick Google after the question reveals that what I was thinking is indeed possible. When I previously worked professionally as an accountant, I used to use this prompt a lot when working in Excel. I know many amazing formulas and ways to utilise Excel, but I also know it has many more functions that I didn't think of searching for until the thought that something like that would be useful. Whenever I was working on something with a lot of data I would always wonder if there was a function that would make it quicker, more accurate, or just better in any way, and there usually was one. I always had this curiosity to wonder how a process could be improved. In comparison, I saw many colleagues never ask these questions and just continue doing things how they have always been done. Sticking with the status quo of what you know and how things have been taught to you can easily happen when you don't allow yourself creative space to dream, or you feel too bogged down with what is on your plate to actually look further out than where you are for answers.

In my business this prompting of playing with what would be cool or great has led to many things being created, and in the back end many processes and systems being simplified to free up more time.

Wouldn't it be great to be a published author? Led me to write and self-publish my first book.

Wouldn't it be great to start an online magazine that covered all the topics I am excited to create around? Led me to be the main creator and editor of a virtual magazine for a year.

Wouldn't it be great if I could wake up naturally (without an alarm), do work that creatively fulfilled me, and felt good about my impact in the world? Led me to many changes.

This prompt has led to many small discoveries and also big changes. This prompt is always the starting point when it comes to the bigger things which leads into more exploration.

Some smaller actions recently have been –

Wouldn't it be great if there was an easy way for me to remember what podcasts I have been a guest on so when I go to update my website I don't have to spend so much time searching and trying to remember? This led me to create a Spotify playlist with all my podcast features, which is so much easier for me to add in as new episodes are released. When I shared that I did this it created a ripple of at least four other people that I saw creating their own podcast features playlist, and them confirming that their inspiration came from seeing me do it.

Wouldn't it be great if some of my private masterclasses were made public on YouTube so more people could find them and I didn't need to go and find the link when people asked for them? I made all my masterclass videos public and then didn't think of it again until less than a week later someone reached out because they found one of my videos from an internet search and wanted to sign on for private coaching.

This prompt helps you to look out into the world for the resources available to you, rather than being stuck in the way you have always done things or the way you have always lived. Often we don't know what is available until we look around.

This prompt invites your creativity in and whenever your creativity is involved, or the more you involve it, the more doors open, the more divine synchronicity lines up, the easier things feel to move through, and the more fun you invite into your life, your work, and your playtime.

Honouring the roots

Playing in the world allows everything you see to be the muse for your creative energy to play and birth new things into the world. When you are taking inspiration from the creative work of others it is important to acknowledge and honour the roots which your creative ideas have grown from.

The way in which you honour the roots, or the source, will differ from creation to creation. It is up to you to hold your own standards of integrity and reverence when it comes to how you communicate your acknowledgements.

There will be some cases where the inspiration or musings come from things that no one has ownership or an original thought claim to. There will be cases where you heard someone say a sentence and that became a musing for an in-depth contemplation to pull from your own wisdom. There will be at times something you see and you want to create something very similar. There will be people you learn from, whose work you want to incorporate into your own teachings or creations. The world is full of creations and you can be inspired by them in many different ways.

Honouring the source will sometimes include crediting another person as the inspiration, and sometimes it doesn't need an external acknowledgement and only an inner reverence.

For me whenever I teach a yoga class I honour the lineage of teachers I learnt from, rarely out loud but always internally. When I have learnt something from another person that I want to talk about I will always acknowledge that I am referencing their work. And there are times when the inspiration was more something that pointed me in a direction and I didn't feel I needed to mention them. It is always different. You need to make the decision for yourself each time your creations hold roots from other creators.

In the world right now there is a lot of talk around cultural appropriation, rightfully so, this is something we need to consider when working creativity. Especially when there are claims of a creation or idea being original when there have been cultures or other groups of people practising what you are sharing throughout said culture's long history.

Speaking on a spiritual level – all ideas belong to everyone; nothing is truly original to one person because all creation came from one Source in which we also were born from.

From a human level and ethical level – you need to be comfortable with your own standards of integrity, there will be many times where honouring the legacy or lineage or creation was inspired from allows it to exist with more integrity. There may be times where you genuinely believe that you were the first person to ever think of something, and it is up to you to discern any due diligence that may be required.

Legally – there are laws in place that you do need to be aware of when it comes to copyright, trademarks, and the likes.

Our creative work can become a mosaic of all we have learnt and experienced. We don't need to credit every single thing we ever say, every time we say it, there is a time and place – while I am not going to fully dive into navigating the nuance of this, what I will say is that I feel it is important for us to have an inner appreciation for where we have come from. Honouring the past, honouring our lineage, and honouring the places that we have been inspired by and infused with our own inner wisdom.

Don't take life too seriously

The final lesson in playing in the world for your creative musings comes from the 46th Gene Key with the gift of Delight.

The shadow for this gene key is Seriousness.

Richard Rudd shares in this transmission of this gene key that "seriousness is the most widespread of all diseases on our planet and is a primary cause of much ill fortune." Richard explains that being in the frequency of this seriousness shadow is like carrying a "black cloud above your head wherever you go," and it always seems "to rain when you don't want it to."

In the shadow of seriousness that black cloud of worry and wishing and expecting focuses your attention on the future or the past, it is always too cloudy to appreciate the moment you could be living. In the dull cloudy view you take yourself out of the divine synchronicity with the world you ought to be living in. It is your seriousness that separates you from love.

Richard also shares that "living without knowledge or memory of the love of the higher planes means that you can *only* take life too seriously." Here a perpetual cycle of seriousness and separation feed each other until you allow your life to be less serious and surrender into love and presence.

Spiritual paths can be taken as seriously as mental and physical paths, all lead to the same shadow cast by the seriousness. Richard shares that the single quality to move out of seriousness and into a higher frequency is "acceptance." "Acceptance equals ownership, which leads to Delight. Delight is the sense of freedom that emerges from an appreciation of the richness of being alive."

The Gift of Delight leads you to "move through the world incredibly smoothly." As it is based on a deeper understanding of life, in that nothing truly matters except for life and love.

If you are in a shadow of seriousness about any aspect of your life, accept this and begin delighting in all around and within you. Taking life too seriously sucks the fun and the juice out of living and can make you blind to all the beauty all around you in the world.

The world being your muse gets to be a fun way for you to play in the world, and for everything you see to be your muse to deeper insights about life, and for your creations to spring through. This isn't possible when you take life too seriously.

Delight in all you see.

The world as your muse: summary

- Get lost in your romantic daydreams about life, and then ground yourself. Your turned-on creative energy from this practice will overflow into all your art.
- Your contemplations open portals of revelations. Give yourself something to contemplate in the background of your daily life, insights will naturally drop in.
- When you feel the intimidation in your body a world of inspiration will open to fuel your action and confidence moving forward.
- The most mundane tasks become artful when you choose to infuse your presence with creative energy.
- Include high contrasting experiences in your life to open yourself to new ideas and energy. The motion of this will create momentum to keep your creative energy fired up.
- You will have many ideas playing in your mind as the whole world becomes your muse. Creating your filter (with questions that fit for you) will help you remain clear of what is for you to create.
- Everything and anything in the world can be the sign that you make it.
- Relax your gaze on any elements within the world to see the art within it.
- Wouldn't it be great if…. any idea you thought of could be brought to life?
- Acknowledge the roots of your inspiration to honour the source in a way that meets your own integrity standards.
- Delight in life by not taking it too seriously.

CHAPTER THREE
YOUR CREATIVE TEMPO

Your story is yours to move through, at your own sacred pace. With the rhythm of the cosmos pulsing deeply in your core, you are divinely in the perfect place.

Sacred Symbolism – the snail

The snail is known for being one of the slowest creatures on earth, seen from the outside as taking an excruciating amount of time to move from one point to another. But what if the snail was moving at the most perfect pace for its own creative evolution?

Fully present to the journey when moving at its slow and steady pace, and when ready to rest, or when it senses it is not safe to move, retreating into its shell. Then coming back into the world and continuing to move.

The snail carries its home on its back. This is the home they are born with, it grows with them in their journey and cannot be replaced.

Just as the snail carries its home with it whenever it goes, so do you. You may live in many different houses in many different places throughout your life, but the only true home you will consistently have is your body. The feeling of home is found in the frequency of love felt in your body. This body of yours grows and evolves with you throughout all the chapters in your story. It can be repaired, it can undergo many changes, but it can never be fully replaced for this life you are living.

The shell on the snail's back contains a spiral that captures the golden ratio, this is a ratio that is found all around us in nature on earth and out in the cosmos. The same golden ratio that is on the snail's shell can be found within budding flowers, sea shells, spiral galaxies, hurricanes, ocean waves, even human faces and fingerprints, and in many other places.

The creation of life is infused with sacredness in each moment, all life is interconnected and interwoven into the fabric of the universe. Interwoven storylines all playing out at their own sacred pace, some slow and steady, some speedy and erratic.

Your own creative tempo and pace will be deeply felt when you ground your base, when you feel home in your body within the interconnected web of the universe. Your natural rhythm is within the divine synchronicity of all life.

Your natural rhythm + divine synchronicity

All creations have their own cycle with phases that they move through. All cycles move at a different pace and tempo. This also applies to you as a divine creation.

Nothing in nature has the same expression in all its moments.

The sky moves from day to night

The moon's earthly glow cycles from a luminous full moon to a dark new moon.

The seasons shift from hot to cold, dry to wet, from preparing the soil to reaping the harvest.

The trees are vibrant and green, the leaves change their colour and then they fall before growing again.

Everything in nature has its perfect timeline, perfect because it is in flow with the rest of the world and all the cosmic forces. And we judge none of it. We don't have any expectation for a seed to bud into a flower overnight. We don't expect the moon to be full throughout an entire month. We don't expect a caterpillar to become a butterfly as soon as they hatch. No, we only place that kind of pressure on ourselves and other humans.

The pressure to force against the universal flow of life.

The pressure to be 'on' and our best at all times.

The pressure to look and act youthful as we age.

When we try to interfere with the universal flow of life we move out of sync with the rhythm and harmony of life.

You live through many phases, there is the overarching cycle of life and death with many phases in between. There are the phases we move through with the seasons, with our menstrual/hormonal cycles (more on this in the next chapter), our creative cycles, relationship cycles, and so, so many others that are personal to you.

The natural rhythm of your overall story of evolution is something of a paradox. It already exists and is available for you to tune into, yet simultaneously, you create it as you live it. Perhaps you creating it is already part of the story that has already been written?

When you are living in your natural rhythm by allowing yourself to fully be in the phase you are in, you harmonise with the universal rhythm. In harmonising you will begin to experience divine synchronicities everywhere you are. You will seem to always be in the right place, at the right moment, in the right mood, with the right people, like the stars are lining up just for you.

This doesn't negate the challenges that help you rise, more like they have been perfectly placed.

Resisting against the natural flow of life takes enormous effort and force. When we convince ourselves we need to work hard to be worthy we can fall into a habit of interfering with life's plans.

We come into a paradox again; you have no control over the events or the storyline of your life, *and*, your actions, creations, and choices all influence the story of your life. There are many elements within your life that you did not choose, and there are many elements that are the results of your actions. The mind can cling to these questions of – am I in control, or aren't I? Am I the creator of my life, or has everything been prearranged? Is free-will and choice an illusion? These existential questions have no answers that will satisfy the logical mind. The answers can only be found within your own wisdom.

The other answer that can only be found in the wisdom of your body is – how do I know when I am moving through life in my natural rhythm?

This is an inner feeling that you will learn to recognise. You will see it externalised with an increase in divine synchronicity.

This synchronicity will be an incredible amplifier for your creativity, the divine timing that unfolds will see everything fall into place just as it should.

As Osho says, "whenever you are in harmony with the natural rhythm of the universe, you are a poet, you are a painter, you are a musician, you are a dancer." And that "All beautiful states are paradoxical. The higher you go, the deeper you go into the paradox of reality. Supreme action with supreme relaxation"

When you are in harmony with the world you are intune with the deeper rhythms of life and creation. The divine synchronicity that unfolds will make you feel like the universe really does have your best interests at heart, and that your creative impulses are part of the universe's divine plan.

Creativity expands time, btw - time isn't linear

Time is not as linear as your logical mind perceives it to be. Some would say that time is an illusion.

There are moments when one hour feels like it goes by quickly, and there are other hours that feel like they will never end. Even though our logical brain argues that the clock ticked the same in both situations, we can accept that our experience of time is different in different situations.

I love the artful exploration of time within the Netflix show, The Good Place. Time moves like 'Jeremy Bearimy,' written in cursive. It loops around and intertwines. The dot above the 'i' is sometimes Tuesdays, sometimes July, and occasionally the time when nothing never occurs. This explanation doesn't make any sense to the human brain so let's not waste energy trying to logically understand it. Rather, let's play with this symbolically and through a quantum lens.

To explore some science behind this concept of time not being linear we can look to Dr Joe Dispenza. I have always accepted this concept intuitively as a mythical idea but it wasn't until discovering his work that I explored how tangible this idea could be. In his book Breaking the Habit of Being Yourself, a study was shared exploring if we could affect the past with our thoughts.

In this book, Dispenza shared a study conducted in 2000 by an Israeli doctor, Leonard Leibovici. This study was a double-blind, randomised controlled trial involving 3,393 hospital patients who suffered from sepsis. In this study half the hospital patients had a group of people praying for their condition to improve. The other half of the hospital patients were not prayed for. The study revealed that the prayed for group showed measurable improvements to their health compared to the not-prayed for group. The time twist in this study; the hospital patients were actually from a list of patients in hospital from 1990 – 1996! The prayers that took place in the year 2000 improved the health of people four to ten years before the prayers were made. Dispenza states that "a statistical analysis of this experiment proved that these effects were far beyond coincidence."

If our prayers can influence the health of a stranger who was unwell a decade ago, it raises the question – was this story already written, that in the future someone would pray for the person whose health improved so their health was always meant to improve. Or, can we change the past? Is there one timeline that changes as we change the past? Or is there a multiverse of shorts with many different possible timelines.

There are many works of art and fiction that explore these questions in different ways. Time travel in the movie Back To The Future is very different to the rules of time travel in the movie Avengers Endgame.

In the work of Dr Joe Dispenza, he explores our influence on distance, space, and time through the Quantum Field. He shares that you can "think of the quantum field as an invisible field of frequency or energy that connects everything physical and material. It is this field of pure energy, which exists beyond our senses, that gives form to this three-dimensional reality." Within this field there is only a forever lasting present moment, he states that "the quantum law says that all potentials exist simultaneously." When we enter this field we can use our mind to create within all of time. As Dispenza puts it, there is "an infinite number of possibilities (that) await the observer."

To have a more symbolic and visual reference for this, we can look no further than the Marvel Cinematic Universe. The Quantum Realm is a big part of the Ant-Man movies, it is described as "its own microscopic universe." In Avengers Endgame, Scott Lang shares that the five years that passed in the real world while he was stuck in the Quantum Realm felt like only five hours for him. He shared that "the rules of Quantum Realm aren't like they are up here… Time works differently in the Quantum Realm." He continues to share his 'what if' thoughts around controlling the chaos and navigating it to enter the Quantum Realm at a certain point in time, to then exit it at another time.

In Avengers Endgame, the Avengers were able to time-travel based on Scott Lang's idea and Tony Stark's invention. They entered the Quantum Realm at one point in time and left it at another point in time, making the past their present and the future to their past. Any change they made in the past would result in a new timeline being created. A completely different view to how time travel is presented in movies like Back To The Future, where changes in the past would impact the present, as they note in the Avengers Endgame movie.

As I have been writing this chapter the first half of the new and final season of Manifest came out (which I binged in two days). In this series there are a number of people who experience what they call 'callings', visions or messages that lead them to different things, usually involving helping someone else or discovering something new in the mystery of the show. In this new season they discovered that their callings were coming from 'divine consciousness' and that when they received a calling, the memory centre of their brain lit up! Their callings are them remembering things from when they connected to divine consciousness.

There are many other movies, books, and other works of art that explore this concept of travelling or moving through time and they all have different flavours for how they explore and the 'rules' that apply.

If you aren't following my movie references that is ok, all of this is to say that the concept of time not being as linear and logical as our minds would have us think, has been explored in many mediums – the creative ideas to explore time in this way are channelled from some cosmic truth, and even though how it is presented on our screens may not be the exact way we experience it in the world we currently live in, our creative interpretations are not meant to be literal.

What if the imagination of the creators of these movies, shows ect. was being channelled from the universe. What if we have experienced all of time already and our imagination is showing glimpses of past experiences?

How would your relationship to your imagination change if you saw it as a memory and not a child-like pastime?

These are not questions that you need to answer. These are questions that we will likely never have a definitive answer that is accepted by all.

It is fun to play in these what ifs. To open your own imagination, using these prompts as portals. What art gets stirred up within you, wanting to be expressed out, when you muse on how time really works?

When it comes to actually applying this to your life and your creative expression, let's look at how creating space for your creativity will create more time for other aspects of your life.

Let's say for example you work a full time job that doesn't allow much space for your creative ideas or expression, maybe go to the gym twice a week, a social event every month, and the rest of the time you are moving through the motions. Life could feel pretty full, like you don't have the space to add much more in.

When you add play time for your creativity into the mix of your life, you expand time by firstly reviving your life-force and moving into a higher frequency.

The impact this has:

- You feel more alive and turned on by life.
- You become more efficient at everything else you are doing.
- You actively seek ways to make more space.
- Your distractions fade away.
- You become a more open channel for all of your creativity.
- Suddenly the issues and problems you face become so much easier to solve.
- Suddenly you are so much more switched on and efficient that you move through both work and home tasks with more pizazz, the dishes, laundry, even cooking is done without the usual dragging of your feet which only drains you even more!
- Suddenly you feel excited to wake up a little earlier and create more time in your morning, and you wake up feeling refreshed.

All of these examples can be logically explained away, but also suddenly these divine synchronistic opportunities open up.

Your creativity expands time.

When I was recovering from burnout, I would spend hours watching Netflix and felt like I didn't have time for anything outside of my top priority commitments. This was a period where I didn't want to have space for more to be added to my schedule.

In a contrasting period of my life, when I was writing my first book, I literally was so excited to jump out of bed in the morning at 6am and write for an hour or two. This is not a common thing for me and there are not many things that would get me up and working on something that early in my average day. My creative energy to write, express, and create that book gave me such a boost in my energy.

Often 'time' or a lack of time is used as a reason for not following creative impulses, but time is as expansive as you allow it to be.

You can be creative with your time as much as you can be creative with all other elements of your art.

The Alpha State

Your brain has changing electrical activity that alters how you experience each moment. Your brain-wave frequency at any given point has a high influence on your experience of time, and on your creativity. In my first book Gentle Glow I explored alpha brain waves and their connection to meditation. In the work of Dr Joe Dispenza, he explores the brain-wave frequencies in much more scientific detail. Meditation, in the right brain-wave state, is how he teaches to enter the quantum field to create from pure energy.

In his book Breaking the Habit Of Being Yourself he describes the different brain-wave states in adults as follows:

Beta – the "everyday waking state" where your brain is "processing sensory data and trying to create meaning between your outer and inner worlds."

Alpha – here your brain is in a "light meditative state" where your "internal world begins to consume your attention."

You naturally come into this state when you are relaxed and limit the sensory data to process (such as closing your eyes). Or when you drift off to integrate information you have taken in, into your memory.

Theta – this is the "lucid state" that you find yourself in when you are "half-awake and half-asleep." Here there is "no veil between the conscious and subconscious minds."

Delta – for most this represents a "deep sleep" with "little conscious awareness." Here the "body is restoring itself."

"When we move into slower brain-wave states, we move deeper into the inner world of the subconscious mind."

The beta brainwave is needed for us to process information in the external world, to get things done, to do all the thinking that is necessary for our survival. Prolonged states in this brain wave is stressful to the body, and whatever is stressful to the body is numbing to our creative impulses. In this beta state we are on high alert for the things we need to do, the things we need to think about, plan, organise, etc. This is not conducive to our highest creativity.

In our alpha brainwave, in our relaxed state, we enter into our highest intelligence, here all the dots connect, the solutions appear, we channel clearly, and we naturally have higher clarity to see and hear what our creative impulses are leading us into.

If you live a 'busy' life and are constantly in the beta brainwave state you may notice that you get your best ideas come through while you are in the shower, or right when you are about to go to sleep. Usually these moments are the first time that you were present and relaxed during your day. These moments are the small pockets where you don't have any active thinking or pressure to figure something out, in this moment your brain waves slower and the ideas and solutions begin to flood. You may remember something that had escaped your mind from earlier, the complexities of a problem could dissolve and a simple solution appear, or new creative ideas drop in.

When you are trying to force yourself through time, often the mental human impulse is to try to do things quicker, to think more, to do more. The irony is that it is actually by slowing down that we get more done, more efficiently and thus in a shorter amount of time.

Your relaxed present state *is* your alpha state.

When you are ahead of your time

Sometimes your creations will be ahead of their time, and they won't be appreciated or used immediately. You may never see others valuing your creations, or you may never receive recognition for your creative contributions.

Two of my favourite stories to highlight this are the creative lives of Hedy Lamarr and Vincent van Gough. Both of their lives and their creative genius is much more remarkable than there is space to share in this book, here are some of the keynotes in relation to how their creative genius was not recognised and celebrated in the world at the height of their creative expression.

The life and inventions of Hedy Lamarr is an amazing example of being ahead of your time and having your art be grossly under appreciated. In her popular days she was known as an actress who created a stir through her on screen nudity and as the first woman to ever perform an orgasm on the silver screen. Her legacy of being the woman to invent the technology that made Wi-Fi possible went unrecognised for most of her life. The Smithsonian Magazine, which is run by The Smithsonian Institution (the world's largest museum, education, and research complex), published an article detailing her life.

Here are some key points -

Hedy Lamarr was an Austrian-born well-known actress in the 1930s and 1940s. She was also an "ingenious inventor who planted a seed that would blossom into some of today's most ubiquitous technology, including Wi-Fi, Bluetooth, GPS, cordless phones and cell phones."

It was noted that Hedy developed an interest in invention when she dismantled a music box at five years old. She let her curiosity keep leading the way.

Her breakthrough invention was made during World War II when she was "trying to invent a device to block enemy ships from jamming torpedo guidance signals." This is how she invented the technology for "frequency hopping." Which would ensure the 'enemy' attempts to intercept messages would be blocked.

When Hedy Lamarr offered her invention to the U.S Navy, they rejected it.

Through the years she continued creating and inventing even into her mature years.

The invention of "frequency hopping" was later shared and begun having widespread use. However, Hedy Lamarr was never compensated. Her patent became expired, and others received public recognition for the groundwork she had laid. She wasn't recognised until 1997 when she was awarded the Pioneer Award of the Electronic Frontier Foundation. Just three years later she passed away at 85 years old. She never made any money from her invention which has an estimated worth of $30 billion.

Her son Anthony Loder was quoted saying that "she would be pleased with the legacy of her 'frequency hopping' concept. She would love to be remembered as someone who contributed to the well-being of humankind."

The life and art of Vincent van Gough became wildly popular after his death, some pieces valued at millions of dollars today, but he only ever sold one piece while he was alive, out of his 800 oil paintings and 700 drawings.

Some notes about his life from Britannica's biography on him -

Vincent van Gough's "artistic career was extremely short, lasting only the 10 years from 1880 to 1890." His most popular works were created in the last three years of his life.

After his death his art became "astoundingly popular" selling for "record-breaking sums at auctions around the world." Van Gough is now considered one of the "greatest Dutch painters of all time." and has become "the most recognised painter of all time."

In your life there may be times where you pour your heart and soul, all of your creative genius, into your work of art and receive no recognition. This underappreciation from others does not make your art any less meaningful. There will be works of your art that are just meant for you, or a more intimate group. And there will be times when you are truly ahead of your time and the wider recognition will come much later in your life, at times even after your life.

Just as some books become wildly popular many years after their release, or some fandoms slowly grow, there are times when it takes fully being in your own creative space to attract a critical mass following of your art.

Just as your creative expression has its own creative rhythm, as too does each of your creations.

In my life there have been many times where I have had sudden creative ideas drop in and shared them with so much excitement to have those ideas brushed off. Then months or sometimes years later the idea would be taken as their own without them realising that I planted the seed. In these cases it was important for me to let go of the thought that I owned ideas before they had been executed or created. It was frustrating, but I kept sharing for years and there were some moments of recognition for how innovative and creative I was.

When you are in an environment that isn't open to change, there will be times when it feels frustrating that your creativity is not embraced. In these situations there isn't anything wrong with you (no matter how hard anyone tries to convince you otherwise) and there isn't anything necessarily wrong with the environment you are in or the other people with it, it is that the creative tempos are operating at different paces.

If you have a face-paced creative tempo then you will feel frustrated at how stagnant some places feel and how slow they move and allow change.

If you thrive in a slower tempo then you may feel frustrated with people who move faster, like they are constantly trying to rush you and push their ideas onto you.

This section is for those who operate a little faster when it comes to their creative energy.

You won't always be recognised for your contributions. You plant seeds so far in advance that when someone suddenly 'has a great idea' they don't even realise that it came from you.

You sometimes just need to leave places that are practically stagnant for your energy.

Your creativity is so important and valuable in the world even when it is not recognised by others as such. You have no control over your art becoming suddenly famous in your old age or after you have left this earth, all you can do is keep creating and enjoy the ride you have.

While you are living and creating, this feeling of being ahead of your time can simultaneously make you feel like you are falling behind.

In one of my favourite Taylor Swift songs, This is Me Trying, her lyrics tell the story of a once high achiever who at some point became burnt out and became someone who felt like they fell behind. She uses such poetic juxtaposition in the story of this song. The protagonist used to feel they were 'shiny' and now they feel covered in 'rust.' They used to feel so far ahead of all their peers until before they knew it, they fell behind and were being overtaken. This journey left them in a place of despair, trying to get help, trying to be better again, trying to understand where they went wrong. This is a song I deeply resonate with, you can pause here to go and listen to the song if you like.

When you are living in this paradox of being ahead of your time and falling behind at the same time, it can feel incredibly frustrating and isolating. It may even feel embarrassing as others see you as 'lost potential.' But know this – you are in the perfect place. Even if you can't see it right now, even if it doesn't feel like it. You are living your story. Your creations are living their own story too. When we detach from what we should be doing, how others should value us or our work, and what ideas belong to us, we liberate ourselves from the heaviness of thinking we should be at any other point than we are in our own story.

Fighting against the rhythm of your story takes you out of the flow of your story, yet you are always right where you ought to be, and there are always other places you can go. What a tangled web. The best part, you get to play in it and create the meaning that you deem as truth.

Sacred laziness – allowing what you do to be enough

The fear of 'not enough time' can become hardwired into our minds and bodies. As humans with a mortal life for our current expression we innately sense that one day we will not be here on earth in the physical body that we are in now. When this fear is kept in the shadows it can become distorted and perverted into a constant fear of 'running out of time' like a cloud that chases us around with its incessant rain.

For all my teenage years and early twenties I felt like this fear was chasing me and I just had to keep up with its pace. It is why I did things like finishing my university degree and professional designation studies in four and a half years, while it was recommended and the norm for those who were working professionally while studying to take at least eight years. And why I was volunteering for around six community organisations at a time, and all the other things. Whatever I was doing, I wanted to do it as fast as possible. I lived by the words 'go hard or go home' and now I can honestly say that if those are the two choices, I'll choose going home every time.

It has taken years of rewiring and re-framing my views on life for me to arrive at a place of allowing what I have done to be enough for the moment that I am in. There are always more things our mind could list off as things we could be doing. Especially now that I am running my business, there are always new ideas to work on, more ways to refine what I have been working on, there are always things around the house that could be done. The list goes on and on.

The word 'lazy' used to have a very strong negative charge for me. Growing up in a house with a lot of people there is always something going on that others in the house think you should be contributing to. Taking a break or wanting some alone time to just do nothing was met with harsh criticism and judgement for me. And there are times when it still is. What I have really grounded into, is that those big reactions are coming from a place of that person not feeling comfortable to rest or to ask for support in a way that is respectful to everyone involved.

I have reclaimed the word 'lazy' as a sacred title. This is very connected to what we explored about the mental pressure to work hard in Chapter One.

There were two pivotal moments for me in my journey of honouring my sacred laziness.

The first was when I realised just how burnt out I was when deciding to leave my professional accounting career. I had a lot of recovery time after this. I was still doing work teaching yoga classes and some casual lecturing, and involved in life, but I spent a lot of down time, it was what my body needed and it was a mental challenge to accept that. There were many moments during that time of my life where I had to numb out the anxiety produced just by thinking I should be doing more and the spiral that took me down. I let myself live in this cycle of nothingness and then a spark ignited within me and I came back into being focused on my business and life with my full power behind me.

The second was when I began exploring my gene keys. The first sequence within the gene keys is the activation sequence, and within this sequence is the sphere of evolution, this is the first 'trigger point' in our profile. It reveals the keys that make up our primary challenge, the shadow we have in this placement can be the most intense shadow for us to face in our journey towards core stability.

In my profile I have the 28th Gene Key with the shadow of Purposelessness in my evolution sphere. Richard Rudd shares in his transmission that "this shadow cuts to the core of the deepest of all human fears – the fear of death."

This is when I was consciously confronted with just how intense my fear of death was which for me manifested as a deep fear of running out of time. This drove me to always want to do as much as I possibly could in the quickest amount of time. Partly what led to the burnout I mentioned earlier. The revelation for me was that in the absence of all the things I was filling my life and schedule with, all that was left was the feeling of purposelessness. I felt like I needed to be *doing* more and more in order for what I felt like would be my short life, to have any purpose.

The reactive side to this shadow of purposelessness manifests as "transforming their fear into activity, they can't stop moving. Their most terrifying space is their own inner silence and stillness."

The song Surface Pressure in the Disney movie Encanto is a beautiful exploration of this shadow of purposelessness, in the movie when Luisa sung "I'm pretty sure I'm worthless if I can't be of service." I was reminded of what it felt like when I was in the thick of this shadow.

But like all shadows, within the shadow of purposelessness there is a gift. Richard Rudd shares that "the fact of death leads us directly to the question of the purpose of an individual's life... we are each born with a creative purpose that no other human being carries."

"If you are to release your true creativity into the world, you must meet your own dark side."

The gift within the 28th Gene Key is Totality. This gift is about embracing the full spectrum of life, all the pleasure and all the pain, while fear walks alongside you in the journey. "This is a path of deep trust in which the individual strikes out on their path, surrendering their whole being into the mystery of life and its hidden rhythms"

Part of my embrace of my gift in this space was the embrace of sacred laziness. Slowing down and fully embracing the pleasures and pain of life rather than speeding through them. This adjustment in my pace of life has been incredible for my creativity and the depth of my work.

Another place within The Gene Keys that gives insight into the divine nature of laziness is the 20th Gene Key.

This gene key has the shadow of superficiality, the gift of self-assurance, and the siddhi of presence.

In the shadow of superficiality you are driven to act and feel as a watered down version of yourself, you live within the illusions of the mind that life itself is superficial and this interferes with your natural deeper connection to life. In this shadow, superficiality manifests as "blind activity for the sake of activity." Blind activity lacks awareness and takes you out of sync with your environment and the natural flow of life.

In the gift frequency of this gene key, you surrender to your trust in life and accept that life has its own flow of plans, when you stop trying to mentally interfere with those plans you fall into a grounded flow with life while feeling assured in your place within life's plans. In your self-assurance you have a higher capacity to make higher frequency decisions, because you are present and your mind cannot distort decisions through premeditating them.

Without mentally agonising over decisions, you make more time available to you. In this gift frequency you allow life to move you, rather than trying to control it with your actions.

Richard Rudd shares that "self-assurance is based upon a philosophy of allowing everything to come to you rather than going out and chasing it down. It is because of this divine laziness that the 20th Gift is the real foundation for inner relaxedness."

The siddhi to this gene key is presence, "the underlying nature of being." Where "pure consciousness floods (your) being, silencing mental activity and drawing (you) into the eternal present moment."

In your divine laziness you allow what is to be enough. In that allowance there is acceptance. In your acceptance there is presence. In your presence there is a divine connection to the forces of creation. You can not predict or plan what will arrive when you surrender to these forces, you can only be present to them in the moment you are in.

Be your own gatekeeper

You are the gatekeeper to your energy, resources, and generosity. Knowing your own boundaries and being able to hold them is a cornerstone to being in your full power of creativity, and also giving in the most potent way.

Your boundaries are not like an electric fence that will zap anyone who dare tries to cross them. Your boundaries are also not a giant stone wall that hides you from anyone trying to get in. Your boundaries are more akin to a gate.

The gate can easily be closed, and just as easily opened. It is up to the gatekeeper (you) what you open your energy to and what you close it to in any given moment.

If you leave your gate unattended, then of course others will let themselves right in. If the gatekeeper is too strict then it can feel very restrictive to whatever is on the other side of the gate to never get any visitors.

The gate and the gatekeeper evolve and adapt with the needs of what they are surrounding.

In business, as an example, there are many situations where others will want your services as a favour (without any intention to give anything back), and it is ok to direct them to your paid offers, or to free content you already have that will answer their question, or sometimes to simply not reply. Behind the gate are all the people in your business that have had some kind of exchange to be there, and if you left the gate open for anyone to walk in and take your attention, it can dilute the experience for those already there.

There will be different kinds of gates holding the space for different things within your life.

Your boundaries are for you. They are not something that you get to force other people to adhere to. There may be people who try to jump over your gate after the gatekeeper tells them to leave. You can create distance from people or situations that you do not feel nurture your energy. And, you can choose to stay present and open hearted in any situation.

Being open hearted, generous, and giving are beautiful qualities, and you also get to have your own boundaries around what you give, when, and how you give it.

In your work and in your life it is ok to gatekeep.

And, it is ok to share generously in a way that feels nourishing to you.

But the expectation that we should share everything is not serving anyone involved.

There needs to be an equal exchange for the energetics of any exchange to feel nourishing for all parties involved. This exchange does not need to be quantified, and it rarely can be in a definitive way.

When it comes to your craft, your creativity, and your art – gatekeep all you want. And share all you want.

The point is that you get to choose.

Over giving is depleting and takes you out of your creative flow.

One of the insights within the 27th Gene Key, which I have in the sphere of my life's work, is that you need to first be selfish before you can be unconditionally giving.

Richard Rudd shares that "the 27th Shadow reminds us of the cosmic forces of creation and destruction. Every Shadow is destructive and leads to death, whereas every Gift leads to life. It is only at the highest siddhic level that life and death are finally transcended."

In the shadow frequency of this 27th Gene Key you can become reactive to selfishness which is about "giving with an agenda" or you can be repressive and become "self-sacrificing."

Your self-sacrificing, which is commonly referred to as 'people-pleasing' is an expression of selfishness because it forces others to take your energy as you become depleted without establishing any personal boundaries. That imposition can often be disguised as altruism. That is until that selfishness is accepted and embraced, and you take care of your own needs. Then you move into the gift frequency of this gene key which is altruism, where giving (after you have taken care of your own needs) is your natural state.

In this gift frequency "giving from the heart can stir up unexpected cosmic forces that work in your favour."

The more you give, the more you receive. But only when your giving comes from a pure place. So go ahead and gatekeep what you need for yourself.

The flow of your evolution

Your life has its own story arc within the cosmic storyline.

There is a paradox that exists. If there is already a story written in the stars, then why does it matter what I do if what is going to happen is going to happen anyway? We can start to get wrapped up in paradoxes and logic loops if we spiral too deeply into this line of thought. It can be intoxicating for the mind to contemplate these types of questions AND you need to choose the point where you stop wondering what you should be doing, and you actually live your life.

You don't need to try to outsmart life, you don't need to prove yourself to others, you can simply choose to be in the moment of your unfolding story.

You get to choose how you feel within your story, and how you move through it.

Getting caught up in wondering what your story is, or how it will unfold, stops you from actually living it.

When you stop trying to interfere with the natural flow and tempo of your life, you get back to living it.

Let the storyline unfold, instead of being stuck in one spot or on a repeating loop.

Your life is a work of art.

Your creative life force wants to write the story of your life, that may already be written by the stars, but regardless you get to live the story like it is the best book in the world being read for the very first time. How exciting!

And once parts of your story have unfolded, you get to look back and frame how you tell your story.

In the playing out of your story there are many ways to get to the same point, so while some critical points may be inevitable there are many paths that lead to that same place. There is space for adventure within your own story of evolution.

You are both the creator and the created. The canvas and the painter. The author and the empty pages.

Your creative energy is what attunes you to the universal flow of creation.

You evolve through your challenges, through your celebrations, through every single experience.

Your creative energy is infused through all of the moments that align you to your story.

Disruption to your rhythm

Just as you think you have found your perfect creative tempo, life could throw a curveball that sends you down some different roads, detours, and into some dark caves that you later find are full of treasure.

Taylor Swift had a beautiful creative rhythm for her first five studio albums, each one being released two years after the last. She would drop the album, soon after she would start to tour that album and in that time write and create for the next album.

But this rhythm was disrupted when she was chased off the internet in 2016. Many believe that there is a 'lost album' from this time period seeing as her last album '1989' was released in 2014. For an entire year Taylor didn't publicly show her face or release any new music right when her fans were expecting a new album inline with her previous creative rhythm.

Taylor surprised everyone when she announced her Reputation album in 2017. Without the disruption that led her to hide away for a year she would not have created the masterpiece (one of my favourite albums) Reputation, and the incredible music video for Look What You Make Me Do.

Falling back into her creative rhythm by releasing the album Lover in 2019, life came in with other plans again. The global lockdowns meant the tour for Lover was cancelled.

In July 2020, less than one year after her last album, Taylor surprise dropped a new album Folklore. Less than six months later she dropped the sister album Evermore! These two albums are viewed by many as Taylor's best work, her most poetic and creative writing, her first albums that fully explored fictional stories in different ways. Without her tour being cancelled indefinitely and being forced into open creative space, Taylor would not have created the space needed for albums like this to take form, at least not in the timing or way that they did.

These unplanned disruptions to her creative rhythm stirred up creative juices and allowed her expression to take new forms, from different parts of her depth.

Something I love about Taylor Swift's music and her approach to writing and releasing it, is how much creativity it stirs up in others! From all the people who have been inspired to sing or write their own music because of her, I love seeing people add their own lyrics to her compositions, to all those who make any kind of fan art, and the way her lyrics can lead you in to connect with your own emotional depth in many ways.

The disruptions I explored here for Taylor Swift don't even include her journey of having her masters sold without having a fair opportunity to buy and own them herself. This wasn't something planned but in following her creative impulse of re-recording all her music that she didn't own the masters to has led to many amazing things for her and her fans. Like all the vault tracks being released, the All Too Well ten-minute version and short film, and bringing new fans into songs she released years ago. Some of her music released decades ago are now being recognised for the masterful songwriting, and absolute bops that they are. Taylor stated that this re-recording journey for her was about "reclaiming (her) art" and that it was part of "the magic and mystery of time and fate."

In your creative journey there will be a time where you will feel like you have found your perfect tempo, and when needed life will come along and throw you off track to get more of your depth expressed out of you. Even when these external disruptions occur, the inner rhythm of your creative impulse is both a grounding and expansive force that aligns you with the overall rhythm of life.

You are always on the right track, even when it feels like you are being taken on a wild inconvenient detour.

The dance of your action

When following your creative impulse into action there is work to be done to bring your creation to life in the world. The work isn't work in the typical sense, more play, but action is needed from you nonetheless.

The more you tap into your creative energy, and the more you open your channel to creative ideas that align with your energy, the more spontaneous bursts of energy you will experience to fuel and guide your action.

While your creative energy can fuel you and energise you any time of day, there will be certain spaces of time that make it easier to get started.

I often tell my clients that once they either turn on the tap, or unkink the hose, the water will effortlessly flow. Rather than waiting at the other end of the hose for water to appear while you remain still. There will undoubtedly be moments where the force of your creation is so strong that it bursts open the tap itself. But for your continued creative action, the first step needs to be made by you.

Once you take your first step and open the flow, creative magic will follow. Joseph Campbell says that "you have only to take that one step towards the gods, and they will then take ten steps toward you."

Explore the days, times, conditions, and environments that are most conducive to you taking your first step in creative action.

If you are a night owl and love to write, draw, play, and work at night – own this. There is this weird superiority complex that many 'morning people' have about waking up early that is reflected in many pockets of the collective. You are not lazy if you sleep in.

You may work best first thing in the morning, or after you have had something to eat. Whatever the case may be for you, make space for your creations in these pockets of time. There may be times that work better for different types of creative tasks. For me I love writing or reading first thing in the morning, and I love doing more graphic related tasks later in the night.

Remembering you are a cyclical being and that the ideal pockets of time may differ from week to week. As you deepen your connection with your body and creative energy, the more you will tune into the best times for you.

There is no rush – spaciousness

When you harmonise the rhythm of life with your own creative tempo a revelation will dawn on you – there truly is no rush.

There is so much spaciousness in the time you have within the moment you are in.

Great insights to this come from the 52nd Gene Key.

The shadow in this gene key is stress. Richard Rudd shares that in the context of the gene keys "stress is a collective pressure and not a personal pressure." The stress we feel when in this shadow is connected to the environments that surround us, we feel the stress in the human auras that are all extending to fill the room they are in. The collective auric body can be the source of the stress you feel in your body.

When the collective is in a state of stress it drives those who are taking on the stress in their own body to stop trusting in the flow of life. Life has its own rhythms and patterns, through its different seasons it naturally knows when to work and when to rest. In stress there is a disconnection to these rhythms which can result in a collapse under the stress, or a restlessness that makes you unable to be still.

The gift within the 52nd Gene Key is Restraint. In this gift frequency you cultivate a deep understanding that nature and life moves at its own pace, in this understanding you restrain yourself from interfering with the speed or rhythm that life is unfolding. You rest in the stillness and peace of truly knowing that there is no rush for anything to move at a different pace to what it is. Richard Rudd shares that in this gift you "accept yourself as part of a far greater flow than you can see" and that "it is through restraint that human power can be harnessed in a creative way." In the siddhi of stillness, you find yourself "sitting at the heart of all creation."

It can be very tempting to interfere when things do not seem like they are working, but remember that every phase is a sacred part of the journey. The pauses, backtracks, expansion points, all of it. Every creation cycle has all of these points and practising restraint to not interfere when from the outside it appears that nothing is moving will bring you into stillness that is nourishing, that will amplify your creative expression when needed. Just because you cannot see the sprouts of the seed does not mean that it is not evolving and growing.

It makes sense when we use the analogy of what we see within nature. When you explore this restraint to your own creative endeavours it can be a little more uncertain what phase you are in or what the next one will be. You do not need to know in order to trust that you are in the right place. Trust your intention. Trust the flow that you are in.

This trust, along with an awareness of different creative phases, allows for great creative stamina. The ability to keep moving and staying in the story while it appears that things may not be working.

The stress of not trusting in the pace of life you are living can have many effects on your creativity and body. In Dr Libby Weaver's (one of Australasia's leading nutritional biochemists) book Rushing Woman's Syndrome she speaks of the 'relentless urgency' that leaves many women feeling "tired yet wired." The need to be constantly moving, and rushing, causes many detrimental changes to your health, and usually leads to burnout. The more stressed and rushed you are, the less space there is for your creativity. If you want to explore the impacts of high stress on your health, I encourage you to explore the books and work of Dr Libby Weaver. Anything that is detrimental to your health is detrimental to your creative capacity. This is not at all to say that you cannot be creative if you are not in your peak condition of health, it is to say that the more radiant your body, the more life-force energy you have access to use in the overflow of your life, and the more space you have for your creative energy to move and express in its natural rhythm.

In 2021 as I was getting ready to launch a new program I reflected on how I had 'failed' in my business more times than I could count. Then the former accountant in me wanted to actually count. It was 13. 13 programs that I created, put together graphics, fully planned out, launched, talked about for weeks, and no one signed up. I thought to myself that I didn't know if I could go through the disappointment of another 'failed' launch. But I chose to trust my creative impulses, and… the number of failed program launches increased to 14. And that was all in a two-year period. Prior to that, there were many events and classes that I had planned that no one booked into, and many that one person attended - sometimes that one person was my mum!

My creative energy gives me stamina, and I trust the process even when I don't know exactly where it is leading me. All my 'failures' in life and business have been fertilisers for magic to grow.

I kept creating.

I kept launching and offering my creations.

None of the bumps or 'failures' were ever really a waste of my energy, effort, or resources. All of these experiences allowed me to gain new skills, to strengthen my processes, to explore more depth within myself, to practise embodying my patience and trust, to create content for the launch that impacted others, to connect with many amazing people through the free events I ran, to tune in deeper to my message and fill all my teachings with so much depth.

Many 'failed' programs became the draft for something else, or elements within it did.

It took me those two years of continuously 'failing' to really relax into my own timeline. In between all these failures were some successes and other opportunities that allowed me to keep pursuing the creativity in my business that I was (and still am) very devoted to.

After the 14th failed program launch it opened space and inspiration to create a free online summit, which went perfectly to my vision. That summit inspired me to create a new short program, which inspired me to create a mastermind, which inspired another short program - which all had amazing women joining and inspired even more creativity within me.

Stress creeps in when we believe there is something wrong with us or that we will never get to the point in our story that we are trying to force ourselves to be in. Keep reminding yourself that every part is sacred, and every phase is part of your epic story. The story of your life would be pretty boring if you skipped straight to the end of every journey within it.

Heed the warning of the Adam Sandler movie Click, where he gets a remote to fast forward through any moment of life. He gets a little too comfortable with this function and before he knows it, he is so far into his story having missed many important parts and inadvertently ruined all his important relationships. He gets the chance to do it all over and realises the importance of fully living all moments.

Stay devoted to fully living your life, in your full creative expression, keep failing forward, stay in your story!

Extend your breath to extend your life

The rhythm of your breath is a reflection of your current life rhythm. Is your breath short and sporadic? Do you sometimes forget to breathe? Or is your breath full, deep, and long?

With our inhale we practise taking in life fully, with our exhale we give back to life. Our breath is such a beautiful example of the cycles of creation. Our breath feeds the trees and plants, which in turn feed us. A constant loop of giving and receiving.

I started to consciously become aware of my breath when I started practising yoga many years ago. I noticed that when I was stressed or rushed I would start to hold my breath and would only notice when I suddenly needed to take in a big gulp of air. Symbolic of how I was trying to force time to slow down to get everything done.

In my yoga teacher training I dove deeply into the practice of Pranayama. Pranayama is a Sanskrit word that can be broken into two parts. 'Prana' means life-force, and 'ayama' means extension.

Pranayama is a practice of controlling your breath, often practising extending and elongating your breath capacity – when we extend our breath, we extend our life.

There are many benefits attributed to meditation – reducing stress, reducing inflammation, improving sleep and brain health, and many other improvements to health. I believe that many of these benefits come from the lengthening of the breath that often accompanies most meditation practices.

In lengthening our breath, we allow our body to activate the parasympathetic nervous system. Giving our body the space to heal from the effects of stress. Our more juicy creativity is conducive with a relaxed state. When our breath is not in harmony with our relaxation and creativity we cannot override this stress in our body with thoughts or force.

Dr Libby Weaver shares that "what activates the parasympathetic nervous system is to extend the length of the exhalations" and "the only way science currently knows how to activate the parasympathetic nervous system, the calm arm (of the nervous system), is to extend the length of our exhalation." She goes on to say that "the only way you can consciously impact the autonomic nervous system is through how you breathe."

Pranayama is powerful with a short regular practice. Three minutes per day is more impactful than a single weekly one hour practice.

A very simple practice is breathing in through your nose, allowing your belly to fill and then your chest. Pause at the top of your breath for one second, and then exhale out through the nose letting the chest fall and then the belly. A second pause holding out the breath and then breathing in again. With each breath elongate the exhale. With a regular practice you will notice your lung capacity expand, and you will begin to notice your natural breathing taking on a new, more spacious, rhythm.

There are many other pranayama techniques, all with different intentions and benefits that you can also explore.

Extending your breath extends your life-force, which extends your creativity. All in a juicy, spacious, relaxed way.

Your creative tempo: summary

- All that lives in the universe has its own divine rhythm, embracing this natural rhythm within yourself attunes you to a divine synchronicity.
- Your creative energy expands time, making more time available for you.
- Your relaxed present state *is* your alpha state.
- Some of your creations will not be appreciated at the time they are created, these creations are still always an important part of your legacy.
- Embrace divine laziness to bring more creative juice into your work and art.
- Your boundaries hold space for more potency in your art and creative expression. Your boundaries are for you. Your boundaries will evolve with you.
- The cosmic storyline of all creation is forever unfolding, you have a powerful story arc within this storyline. Your evolution is part of the collective evolution.
- There is no rush. You have space. You have time. When you stop trying to interfere with life's natural timing, you make more time and creativity available to you.
- Your breath is your most powerful tool to harmonise yourself with the creative forces of life.

CHAPTER FOUR
WOMB WISDOM

Within the darkness, within the void, much is created and much is destroyed. In this womb we will find this constant cycle of life and death, in our womb it is where we hold our truest depth.

Sacred symbolism – the moon

The moon holds so much sacred symbolism, and so much beautiful magic. The moon moves through phases, each just as beautiful as the others. When the earth is between the moon and the sun, the sun shines on the moon for us to see it shine in a luminous glow lighting up the night's sky. When it is the moon between the earth and sun, we don't see the reflected light and our sky is filled with darkness. With the many waning and waxing phases in between revealing just parts of the moon to us.

The high and low tides of the ocean are influenced by the moon with its magnetic pull-on water. With our human bodies being made up of at least 60% water it stands to reason that the moon has an influence over us as it moves through its different expressions.

The word 'lunatic' originated from the wild crazy-ness that accompanies the full moon, along with the myth of werewolves. The full moon is also the time linked to ovulation, where the hormones within are ready to fuck and become with child. Perhaps ovulating women were at the core of the werewolf mystery?

The new moon is associated with our time for bleeding, an inner retreat where in the dark we see more clearly, a time for us to connect with our inner wisdom through solitude.

The beautiful moon is a reminder in the sky that we too move through many phases, all as sacred as the others. All expressions have their place within cycles of our creations.

There are 13 lunar cycles in a year, and on average menstruators bleed through 13 cycles in one year. Throughout history the number 13 has been vilified and re-branded as 'bad-luck' however this number has sacred links connected to the celebration of the divine feminine. The number 13 is also the Death card in Tarot, a card which in modern times can generate some fear. But as we have explored, death and destruction are a sacred part of creation. Death can signal new beginnings and new creations, every ending is a new beginning.

We hold the energy of the moon within us, in our womb space (whether you have a physical uterus or not). This is a powerful energy point for our creative energy.

13 drops of wisdom from the womb

We cannot have creation without the womb.

That is the creation of physical human life, and of energetic creative life.

The structure and functioning of a physical womb holds sacred codes and lessons that we can apply through our creative journey, our biggest creative journey being our entire life.

Through this chapter we will explore 13 sacred drops of wisdom that we receive through our womb and all parts that connect to the womb.

These lessons and codes are symbolic, you can think of them coming directly from your own womb or from the universal cosmic womb. All feminine identifying beings have a strong connection to their inner womb space (some may call it their sacral chakra or their yoni) whether you have a physical uterus or not. This applies if for whatever reason your uterus has been removed or you were never born with one, or whatever your experience has been. It doesn't lessen your connection to your energetic womb.

To preface this entire chapter, I encourage you to take everything that is explored symbolically or metaphorically. The drops of wisdom are symbolic lessons the womb is sharing with us to juice up our creations on earth. Within this chapter I include the physical functioning of the womb and talk about sex, birth, miscarriage, and many other facets. If any of these words or topics do not sit well with you to explore in this way you are welcome to substitute them for different words or to skip over those parts. Of course actual children do not have the same meaning or value to us compared to our creative babies, this entire chapter uses a lot of romanticised poetic language.

Some of the parallels I draw may not connect directly back to your personal experience, this is where you can stay with the symbolic lesson or feel into your own unique womb wisdom.

1. Breathe before anything else

Life begins with the breath. When we emerge from our mother's womb we become animated in our human form with our first breath. As we breathe life in, we activate our own life-force and it begins flooding our body. This life-force pulses through your body until your final breath.

Our stability and foundation of safety begins with the breath.

We learn our initial breathing pattern while we are still inside our mother's womb, in the womb we are held and supported, growing to the rhythm of our mother. If we inherited constricted breathing, we do not need to blame our mother, she did the best she could at the time, it is up to us now to re-parent and re-stabilise ourselves as needed. As we move through life there are many other forces pulling us down into constriction, this begins with the initial separation from leaving the womb, the holy ground of the primal sacred wound that we all carry a piece of. As we live our lives there are many things that trigger the pain of this sacred wound, if we remain closed we create fog and shadows around our light, if we allow the pain to crack us open, we allow more light through and out. The difference between these two experiences is in how we breathe in the moment.

Short and shallow breaths create more constriction. Long, slow and deep breaths allow for expansive opening and presence.

As you take in a deep breath, your belly expands. Bring your hands to your womb space and visualise this space being flooded with golden light with every breath. Create safety in your relationship with your body, your womb, and your breath.

2. Sacred boundaries

Your cervix is the sacred gatekeeper to your womb, sitting between your vagina and uterus. Nothing can enter or leave your womb without the permission of your cervix. As this sacred gatekeeper, your cervix holds the codes of setting sacred boundaries.

Your boundaries can be gentle, loving, and flexible, rather than forceful and rigid. Your boundaries serve the purpose of prioritising your life-force above all else. Just as your cervix serves the purpose of prioritising the highest good for your womb.

The cervix produces mucus that either acts as a protector of sperm or a barrier to that sperm entering the uterus. It creates the boundary only when needed.

During pregnancy the cervix produces mucus that forms as a plug to protect the baby from potential infection. It creates distance between what is to be nourished from what could potentially cause harm.

During childbirth the cervix softens and opens (dilates) to around 10 cm to allow the baby to be birthed into the world. It is flexible to move as our needs move.

Your boundaries are the distance you have between yourself and other people or things. You get to decide that distance (physically, mentally, emotionally, energetically) and you get to hold that space for yourself with love. You cannot project a need for boundaries onto others, you can only hold them for yourself and act in reverence to yourself when the distance you are keeping is crossed. You get to decide the consequence to your boundaries being approached or crossed and it is always your responsibility to take on that consequence whether it be more distance or action being taken.

You get to decide the distance you need to keep in order to love something or someone fully. Sometimes that is very close and sometimes a lot more distance is needed. You get to honour your needs. While you cannot control other people, you do have sovereignty over how you respond.

Your cervix only responds to the situation as it arises, it has no control or influence on the moments preceding the gatekeeper action needing to be taken.

Your boundaries do not create an electric fence that keeps everyone out or hurts them if they get too close, your boundaries are like your cervix, adaptable, in rhythm with your needs, and in high service to your life-force and your heart.

3. The duality and union of creation: masculine and feminine energy

The womb is where duality merges into cosmic creation.

Both energetically and physically.

All creation in the world is formed through the cosmic orgasm of the feminine and the masculine coming together. The two analogies I love to use when exploring the synergetic relationship between the divine masculine and divine feminine are of the river, and the car.

The river is made up of the riverbed; the land, structure, and shape, and the water that fills it. The riverbed in and of itself is sturdy, strong, space, by itself it is a big hole in the ground that serves no purpose. The water inside of the riverbed is flowing, soft, also with great strength, it is life providing and magical in many ways. Without the structure of the riverbed, the water would lose its power and potency as it dissipates by being spread too thin with nowhere to be held. Both elements are needed for the full expression. Neither more important than the other. The riverbed is the masculine, and the water is the feminine.

The car is metal, mechanical elements and a nice thing to look at, the fuel is needed for the car to serve its purpose to move and drive. The physical car is the masculine, the fuel is the feminine. The fuel alone has nothing to bring to life. Both are needed for the full expression of the creation of the car.

The masculine is consciousness, time, and space.

The feminine is energy, movement, flow.

Your womb is a powerful space holder to these dual forces to become one so that something new is created in their union.

Just as the sperm and egg merge into new cells that eventually form the new life of a baby inside of the womb – the masculine and feminine forces in the cosmos merge together energetically in your womb when you are the sacred human to bring that creation to life in the material world. Your 'creative babies' are energetically conceived in your womb.

The energetic story of the riverbed and the car are playing out inside of your womb, you are preparing for new life to enter the world. It will be born through you when it is ready.

You have had countless creative babies with the universe, and they are all still off living their creative life having been born from you.

You hold both feminine and masculine within you, in this duality you can play in either energy in different experiences. When there is union, there is wholeness, there is unity, there is creation.

4. Inner seasons of life

Your womb governs your inner seasons.

You internally cycle through winter (typically when bleeding), spring, summer (typically when ovulating) and autumn, and around again and again. Whether you physically have a menstrual cycle or not, you energetically cycle through the seasons. Your inner cycles may be completely different to another's, but we all experience all the seasons nonetheless. Women and primarily feminine beings are designed to be cyclical beings. We are not the same expression of ourselves from one season to the next, let alone one day to the next. Whereas masculine beings tend to be more consistent with their energy from day to day.

Each inner season is represented by a divine feminine archetype that we can call upon and embody, to support us to live in each season to its highest nature and expression. As we move through our life cycle, coming into the age connected with these archetypes, our relationship to the different archetypes may shift and evolve. Regardless of your age, you hold the codes to the maiden, mother, enchantress, and crone within your womb.

The inner seasons and archetypes

Spring – Maiden – Waxing Crescent Moon: the young energetic woman who gets things done and has fun while doing it. Life is all about play and productivity. She is young and flirty, maybe a little naïve, but she has big dreams and is very willing to do the work needed to get what she wants.

Summer – Mother – Full Moon: the caretaker, the nurturer, the woman who lovingly takes you into her heart with the biggest hug. Also, the protector, she is kind and gracious until her young (or creations) are threatened, then she does not hold back in standing up for those she loves. She can hold so much, and she can look at things the maiden began creating and add to them with more creative depth. She is like water, soft like a flowing stream but also strong when she needs to be.

Autumn – Enchantress – Waning Crescent Moon: the wild woman who does not give a fuck. On the outside she seems unpredictable, internally her energy can feel like a rollercoaster, but she deeply honours her inner rhythm and anything that does not serve the highest good is immediately cut from her life. She carries great and potent creative power that serves as the fire to destroy anything that needs destroying, and to pour magic into whatever rises from those ashes.

Winter – Crone – New Moon: the wise old woman who seeks stillness and solitude. She is highly attuned to her divine nature, the most spiritually aware. Divine wisdom is easily accessed when she rests into her being. She is preparing to die, she is at peace knowing and trusting she will be reborn.

Honour your own experience of these seasons, in life there are cycles within cycles and there are times when our inner cycle is out of sync with the external cycle, there may be times when one season is a whirlwind and others drag out. Your experience of a certain season may be different to how another experiences it. Whatever the case is for you, tune into your own inner rhythm, your own experience of the seasons within you.

You are not designed to be the same everyday, you are a cyclical being. You have access to different skills and gifts during different seasons and phases. Feel each of your divine feminine archetypes through their season within your womb.

5. Beauty in the void

There is darkness until there is light.

There is silence until there is sound.

There is nothing until there is something.

The void isn't empty, it is alive with all that is and ever could be at once, simply being until called to birth something fresh and new, in this way the void is pregnant with potential. But the void puts no pressure on itself to attain or achieve, or to be productive in any way, it rests in its being.

Beauty is born from the void.

Your womb is the void in your body, the empty space that holds the space for beauty to be born and emerge into the world from.

Your womb invites you into the cosmic void. With deep trust that the darkness is sacred, that the silence is serving, that beauty and creation will always emerge from the nothingness.

It is the emptiness in the void that all creative ideas are born from. Delight in the void. Admire the beauty that emerges.

Do not apply force or pressure, this only gets in the way of you resting in your being. The new will always emerge from the void, when you trust this truth, you rest easily in the moments between.

When you rest easily in the moments between, your entire life becomes your work of art that is reflective of your inner essence.

The 1st and 2nd Gene Keys share much about the sacredness of emptiness. Richard Rudd shares that the 1st Gene Key is seen as "the primary code for all creative life in the universe" and the 2nd Gene Key the "primary code for directing all creative life in the universe."

In the gene keys the shadow and the siddhi give birth to each other. The shadow of the 1st Gene Key is Entropy. "Entropy is a measure of the disorder or unavailability of energy within a closed system. More entropy means less energy available for doing work." "Entropy is the black hole to creativity's white hole." It may then sound contradicting to explore how "the secret to harnessing creativity actually lies in the 1st shadow." But that is part of the beautiful paradox within the Gene Keys transmission, and within life itself. "Entropy and creativity are an eternal dance played out within the universe"

Whenever you allow yourself to be in the darkness of your lower frequencies and then proceed to move through them harnessing the energy (but not attaching to it), you re-enact the creation myth of the 1st Gene Key "out of the darkness suddenly light emerges." "This first Gift is called the Gift of Freshness because whatever emerges out of its numbing chemistry is absolutely new." "Out of every dark hole into which you dive comes forth a sally of starling and profound creativity."

The 1st gene key holds to storycodes of the divine masculine, while the 2nd gene key holds the storycodes of the divine feminine that grounds all stories into the world of form.

The 2nd Gene Key teaches us that "at no point in evolution has anything ever occurred that was not part of a huge, interconnected plan." This gene key shares that all life is choreographed from a force that is within the universe, and found inside of you.

"All human life follows the same archetypal pattern laid down inside your DNA. Evolution itself is drawing you inexorably along the path towards awareness of your unity and oneness"

The Gift of the 2nd Gene Key is Orientation, a direct manifestation of this gift is synchronicity. This gift allows you to "peep through the keyhole of existence and place yourself in a wider perceptual context." "Synchronicities cannot be forcibly created but flow out of the feminine nature of the 2nd Gift – in other words, they happen when you are not looking."

Rest in the void, rest in the darkness.

When you find yourself there, trust you are exactly where you need to be in that moment, in that breath.

6. Your sexual energy, creative energy, and life-force are all one in the same

Revisiting something we covered in Chapter One, your sexual energy, creative energy, and life-force energy are all one in the same. This energy is sourced from the same unending reservoir in your body – your womb space.

The different words we use for this same energy may alter the surface level act or experience being energised, but they are all the same nonetheless.

We cannot suppress one and not the other.

We cannot energise one and not the other.

They are all one in the same.

To reclaim or embrace your sexuality is to become more creative. Just as to suppress or deny your sexuality literally and metaphorically dries you up.

To experience pleasure is to get your creative juices flowing.

To feel alive with your life-force flooding your body is to enhance your sexual experiences and your creative expression.

What is your relationship with your sexuality?

What is your relationship with your creativity?

Do these questions yield different responses?

If any distortion has taken place, the centre for healing is within your womb.

You are here to birth new life into the world, this new life can take many forms. Through your physical sexuality you can birth new humans, through making love with the universe you bring new creative life into the world. It is your life-force that drives this impulse of creation, to perpetuate life in all forms. Not just human life but the cosmic life that is God or the Universe or Source living through us.

7. Prosperity is your birthright

You are abundance itself.

Living prosperously is your birthright.

The manifestation and material experience of prosperity is different for each individual human being. We all have different requirements and different designs for what we need and want. You hold the coding within you to be the most prosperous version of you, in whatever form that takes.

The sacral chakra governs prosperity, and its material form, money. Your connection to your sacral chakra, which resides in your womb space, influences your magnetic pull and receptivity.

How open do you feel to receiving?

Feeling constriction, tightness, or disconnected from your womb can in turn prevent you from receiving the prosperity that is your birthright to hold and have flow through you.

Look at the ways in which you prevent yourself from lovingly receiving, whether that be compliments, gifts, money, love, and notice how it feels in your womb when you deny yourself this flow of prosperity.

When you receive, you give. When you give, you receive. You can never take too much; nature will always find harmony in this infinite loop of giving and receiving. Rest in your place within this loop.

Prosperity is your natural state, it is your birthright.

All too often money is tied in with creativity in a way that it shouldn't be. Yes, there are practical logistics to navigate and real human responsibilities when we consider the things we pursue and have access to in our life. There are also universal truths that aren't always helpful to hear when you are in survival mode. The nuance and complexities of this reality are not something I will make space for within this book but know that all is valid.

You are wildly creative. You are wildly prosperous. Simply by existing. Your creative energy, and thus sexual energy, opens you to be more receptive to life penetrating you with prosperity.

8. Your emotions are divine signals

The womb is empty space (outside of pregnancy) within the body. This energetically makes it the perfect space to store suppressed energy and emotions.

Emotions are simply energy in motion within the body. Emotions are to be felt and expressed. There for us to experience the full spectrum and depth of life. Our emotions can be divine signals for us through our life when we honour them (rather than suppressing them.)

When we refuse to feel, express, or listen to the signal of this energy, it becomes stored in the body. The energy finds empty space where it can, like within joints, and within any empty space that can be found – the womb is gold real estate for this storage.

When this emotional energy is stored it becomes a heaviness in the body, leaving an energetic charge connected to certain triggers. Those triggers can be memories, relationships, words, thoughts, anything we take in with our senses. With the charge attached it is difficult to see through the fog to the message of the emotion. The emotions then become compounded and can spiral into destruction or perverted creations.

Our emotions can be beautiful fuel for our creations, or they can haunt us into destruction. Emotions are governed within our womb space in their original form.

Emotions will be explored more deeply in Chapter Six.

9. The pulse of your clit is guiding you into a deeper flow with life

The pulse of your clitoris aligns you to the pulse of the earth. The pulse of the earth draws you into flow with creation. Many of us have distorted views when it comes to the functions of our body and what that means about us in the moment certain sensations arise. Arousal in our body is not always sexual in nature. It is very normal to feel a little pulse in your clit when you are excited about something happening in your life, when you are having an amazing time with friends, when you are in awe of life, or when you solve a problem that has been annoying you for days. These moments, even though they may seem unrelated, open you up creatively because that is what happens when you are naturally enjoying life. The pulse of your clit is a sensation of your intuition, your divine instincts becoming one with your primal instincts, and when you trust this sensation within your body (rather than shaming it in any way) you can begin to follow the guidance of this pulse.

10. Your darkness is sacred

Our womb is the ultimate divine symbol for the cycle of fertility, death, and rebirth. This *is* the cycle of creation. Often we attach negative and fear based meaning to 'death' and darkness. When I speak of death in the creation cycle we can look at it both literally and symbolically.

As we have explored; the shadow of creation is destruction. The shadow is just as sacred as the light. Without destruction there can be no creation. Your darkness is just as sacred as your light.

A lean too far into either pole can take you out of the natural flow and can distort the sacredness of either destruction or creation. Even though your capacity to destroy is sacred, there are times when it is unhelpful and acted upon with ill intentions. Your intention and your energy within each moment of the creative cycle is what determines how aligned any one action is. This is to say that just because something appears to be destructive from the outside, doesn't make it bad. And just because something looks creative from the outside doesn't make it good.

The divine feminine is full of contradictions, paradoxes, and irrational, wild energy that can't ever make logical sense. This part of you, even when it appears dark, is always sacred and a divine part of all creation in the world.

The Hindu Goddess Kali is one of my favourite mythical stories when it comes to the embrace of our own darkness. I wrote a poem about her for my last poetry book, Vineyards of Honey, and have shared it here with you here -

Kali – the goddess of death

Death, doom, destruction
An embodiment of the feminine divine
And the manifestation of anger
Yet her violence engenders no crime
She is more than death
For it is she who clears the space
For new cycles of creation
To come and take their place
She is raw and she is wild
It is not in her nature to be tame
Introducing the goddess of death
Kali is her name
She has four arms and hands
One carries a sword dripping red
Two hands are together blessing her devotees
The other holds a decapitated head
Around her neck is a reminder
Of the darkness she has consumed
A necklace with more decapitation on display
Some say her presence means you're doomed
She devours
She destroys
She plays with the corpse
Like they are toys
Her wild energy is needed
To destroy what lurks in the dark
To dismantle and clear the ground
Before new creation can spark
Once upon a time
Dark forces were dominating all around
She went into a fiery wild fury
And started to burn the whole world to the ground
Enough action was taken
But she could not be tamed
Until her lover stepped in
And she killed him all the same
For this she showed great remorse

But it was too late
Her lover was dead beneath her feet
Was this his final fate?
This shock broke the trance of anger
She entered a new state of calm
She breathed new life into her lover
And welcomed him back into her arms
Kali is within you
A force to be wildly destructive
But she is never unprovoked
Her anger is productive
She destroys
She will dismantle
Her actions
You can always handle
She may seem irrational
But this is just her divine play
Her energy is sacred
Will you allow her to stay?
Without death and destruction
There can be no new life created
Kali, she who is death
Will be here even when she is hated
She knows her place in the cosmos
To fertile the soil in the ground
Again and again and again
So the new can be found.
Take her story as symbolic
So your dark forces do not continue to grow
Can the embodiment of Kali
Help you destroy what needs to go?
Don't be afraid to be irrational and angry
To embody your feminine force
To clear the space for the new that is calling
And for you to connect deeper to your Source

11. The sacred ancestry

Part of you existed within your grandmother's womb.

When your mother was in utero, she had all the eggs she would have for her lifetime within her ovaries. The egg that would one day become fertilised and then become you was inside of your maternal grandmother.

This ancestry may continue with you, if you do carry a baby within your uterus, who then grows and gives birth to another human – the seed of that human, your grandchild, was within you while you were pregnant.

We have a deep connection to our ancestry within our body and through our blood, even if there was no physical presence within our lives.

It can be juxtaposing to consider the lives lived by those in our lineage line, the different challenges they faced, the trauma they may have endured. Consider how this all may still be present within your bloodline, from the trauma stored in the body passed down by blood, to generational wounding projected onto family members.

A couple of years ago I wrote a book exploring the life of my Nonna, even though I knew the keynotes it was illuminating to hear her retell all she experienced in her childhood, from living in Italy as a child and teenager needing to work and look after her younger sister, to leaving her home to come to Australia, and all that happened since arriving in this country. Her full story is not mine to retell in this book. What I encourage you to do is to make the time and space to explore your ancestry, and speak to your parents and grandparents about their lives. Make art out of it if that feels fitting. If you do not have blood relatives, use your imagination to play with what their lives may have been like.

We have a sacred ancestry, and this sets many paths we will travel on throughout our lives.

In The Gene Keys it is shared that our core wound is imprinted while we are within our mother's womb. Your mother's core wound was imprinted while she was within *her* mother's womb. Our core wound is our slice of the Sacred Wound, the collective karma that we take on to transcend. This is something that we are born with, this wounding will manifest into shadows in our lives regardless of how we are raised or the life we are born into, while these elements can influence how it manifests into our lives, it will manifest nonetheless. There is a lineage of wounding within our blood that is infused into us while we are in utero.

You may be the sacred woman who heals for your entire ancestral line. There are spiritual teachings that share when you heal, you heal seven generations back and seven generations forward (remember time isn't linear from Chapter Three).

In The Gene Keys, this core wound is what becomes our Vocation, our highest service in the world, the parts that hold the heaviest shadows, contain the most light within the gifts. This is explored deeply within the Venus Sequence of The Gene Keys.

12. The parallels between the creation of; human life and creative life

There is a great poetic parallel between human life being created and birthed into the world, and how creative ideas are materialised and birthed into the world. As we explore this analogy here I am going to use the example of creating a book that you wish to birth into the world. Use your imagination to apply it to any of your creative ideas.

First comes the attraction, seduction, flirting, and foreplay. Life wants to turn you on, life wants to seduce you to delight in being alive. The more alive you feel in your body, the more radiant your life-force and the more attractive you become to all the creative ideas flying around in the world. This is about getting wet and lubing up. There is no commitment in this stage, it is about sampling all that you delight in within the world. There will come a point where you are ready to take things to the next level, to enter into a commitment of sorts.

In the example of creating your book, this is where you begin playing with the idea of writing a book, no details are set in this phase, it is all just playing and fantasising while the universe pulls you deeper into your desire to be an author! You may think of this desire every time you see a book, every time you see someone else publish their own book, the universe will flirt with you using whatever turns you on the most around writing your own book.

Then comes the union, the **making love with the universe** if you will. Allowing life into you. The cosmic orgasm of creation takes place as you embrace the full pleasure of this explosive moment. There may be times where this feels a little overwhelming and you just want to rush it out, get it done with! Bring presence in this moment to slow down, surrender into the moment, know that you can hold this expansive energy in your body and you can feel every moment of it. Surrender into the void the orgasm melts you into.

This is the commitment to your book, the union of your energy with the universe's energy. You may open a word document and type your first words, you may make the declaration to someone close, you may know the title or core topic of your book in this moment. In this moment the book begins to feel real, rather than just a pipe dream. There is much excitement in this moment where everything feels like it is all coming together.

When you start making love with life, you may also begin to anticipate or desire yourself to become pregnant with a creative idea that you get to bring into the world. You may start taking your symbolic prenatal vitamins, you may start creating space in your life, you begin to prepare in any way that you can.

This preparation for your book could look like taking a creative writing class, researching 'how to write a book', maybe you hire support from this early stage, it would be that you start playing with the vision without firm details yet. You may set up your writing space, or do anything that brings you into the energy of possibly getting pregnant with your perfect book idea.

Following this poetic analogy, **next comes the conception**. The fertilisation of your metaphoric egg with the universes' metaphoric sperm.

From this moment you begin to connect with the creative soul of your book, you start to open your energy to seeing and receiving all the synchronicity you need to bring this book to life. Your pregnant glow calls in all you need. Like the perfect support or editor, the perfect words to begin forming your thoughts.

There are times when the creative idea was not meant to come to be in our life, and we have an energetic miscarriage. There will be a period of time we need to grieve and let go of the hopes and dreams we had for that idea to be in our life. We will all have a different experience of how we process this loss.

Or you **hold the energy of our creative baby as it grows within** you. You begin to channel the creative soul of your creation to ground its being on earth.

There will be a moment in time when the energy of your commitment to your book is just for you. You get to hold the idea, feel the glow of your excitement, and embrace all that you begin to channel. Holding this potent and expansive energy can sometimes stir an overwhelm, especially if our mind begins to attach to the moment of time we need to hold this idea before it comes into the world, or before we even feel ready to share it with others. This is the time to practise holding big energy in your body.

We start **letting the excitement build**, mentally and emotionally preparing it to come into our lives. We start to let our inner circle and select people in on the news of what is coming. We start to form our support team for all aspects of the birth and life. The wider announcement is made when you are ready, sharing the details that feel good to share.

For your book, you may announce that a book is coming without sharing any details, you may even share the expected date range it will be in the world. You may have a 'gender-reveal' of sorts by sharing the book title or cover before it is fully born. You may start inviting people to the baby shower to celebrate right before the birth, with a book party or press tour. Everything is being planned, organised and put in place in the background while you share what you decide to with others.

While you are pregnant with your book your energy needs will likely shift, metaphorically (and sometimes literally) you will start 'eating for two' as they say. Writing extended exerts a lot of energy from the mind and uses your energy in a new way. You may find yourself having cravings, needing to take more breaks than you normally would. There are many changes, some subtle and some abrupt, that you will notice within your body. All of this is such a natural part of the process.

Then comes **the birth**, perhaps planned or perhaps it happens suddenly when the time is right.

You may set a release date for your book and have everything in place for it to be officially published on that date, and a few weeks early you spontaneously feel the urge to release it early. The birth of your book is when you launch it into the world, it is published and ready to meet all those who want to read it.

Your creation has taken form in the world, in a way detached (but still connected) to you. In this form your creation can be interacted with, with your presence. **Your creation will begin to form independent relationships in its sovereign life**.

When others buy and read your book they have a connection with your energetic transmission, along with your words, that is separate from you. Your readers will have varying experiences and interpretations of your book. Your book will begin taking on a life of its own where it inspires, influences, and impacts people in many different ways.

After the creative birth it is time for a lot of **self-care, inner**

nurturing, support where needed, and really honouring the energetic low that will likely follow the big exertion of energy and creative life-force. In the pregnancy there was this continuous feeling of fullness, after the birth it is natural to feel a moment of emptiness.

It is very common after a big creative project, like writing a book, to feel depleted in energy for a moment after its creative birth. While writing your book you were an open channel, and you exerted energy in your writing and all other components. This takes a toll on our human bodies, and your body will need time to rest and recharge after this experience.

The experience of writing your book likely gave a sense of fullness in your life, filling your mind and heart with ideas on what to write about, what to add, filling your schedule with writing and editing time, and all the other elements of creating your book. Once the book has been birthed, empty space opens around you.

In this moment honour the emptiness, for there is fullness within the emptiness. Fill the space with your love for the creative journey, while you honour the space needed to recharge and rest in the void.

During your journey of writing your book, it likely held a mirror to your inner world. Especially if your book shares your own story. It can be a vulnerable and also an incredibly healing experience when you allow it to be. There is space needed after the birth of your book to digest, absorb and integrate all you have experienced in the entire journey to keep your energy grounded.

While your creation is a baby you begin **to co-parent with the universe**. In this stage of your creation's life, you are the primary decision maker. You can trust that the soul of this creation chose you as its guardian, it has full trust in your decisions, you can trust the moves you make. The universe is a loving co-parent looking out for the wellbeing of this creation too, it is not all on you.

After your book is published and available in the world, there are still actions required by you to take care of it, you will promote it, talk about it, likely support others who are reading it. And you will have the support of the universe to carry its transmission and line other people up in their own divine synchronicity to find your book.

While you are co-parenting your book in its infant stage it can be tempting to bring another creative baby into the world right away. Imagine having two babies back within weeks or months of each other! In this time focus your energy on your creation that exists, while still holding the desire to inevitably birth another.

Your creation begins to grow up into a toddler, teenager, and full-grown adult. Over its life gaining more and more independence from you. You still hold a sacred connection with this creation coming into the world through you, but there will come a point where it has interactions and relationships, and impact in the world with no involvement from you. It will take on a life of its own. People will interpret it in different ways, perhaps praising it, perhaps criticising it. None of this is for you to take personally, although you may step in to defend it when you feel called to.

As your book has been out in the world you will have less active involvement with it, it is still something that you honour, recommend to others and celebrate, but it won't be at the forefront of your mind always, and it will take a backseat to other books and other offers.

There is no predictable timeline when it comes to our creations for when they will move into each developmental phase. Each creation moves to its own timeline. Some may be in the toddler phase for years and years, while others grow to be an adult very quickly.

Your creation may even form a union with another creative force and birth something new, in a way you become a creative grandparent.

Someone may write fanfiction based on your book, someone may use quotes from your book in their own creation, someone may start a book club with your book, someone may approach you to see if they can use the content of your book to teach to others, there are many ways others can create a union between your book and their creative energy.

There may come a time when you completely end your role in the creative life of your creation, there may even be times when this creative life doesn't get to fully grow and you decide to let it go. Even when this is the case, the transmission and the impact of this creation lives on.

Down the road you may feel less aligned with the first book that you ever wrote, this doesn't dilute the power of its creative transmission, it will just see you dissociate with it. There is a popular author whose books are owned by her former publisher and still circling in the world even though she actively encourages all who have her books to destroy them. While this may taint the experience of reading her books for some, it doesn't change the impact her books have had in the past.

Playing within the analogy of this poetic parallel can help you tune into the rhythm of creation within the universe more deeply. To fully be in the phase you are in and to settle the mind in knowing part of what is coming.

Reflecting on how you have flowed through this process with our previous creations can reveal great insight into the relationship you have with life and the universe.

13. You hold so much more depth than you are raised in this world to believe

You are far stronger than our modern world raises us to believe. You are also far softer. You are both. You have an immense capacity to hold the depth of the full spectrum of life.

Childbirth is a concept that blows my mind whenever I think too much about it, how humans come to exist in the world and continue to grow into adults. It is wild to my logical mind. And it is deeply sacred.

When in childbirth the contractions of the womb help to open the cervix 6-10cm. In this natural experience you are stretched beyond what seems bearable, yet you bear it. In the contractions of your uterus you are squeezed and taken into symbolic darkness, right before you expand and open into light.

Often in our creative journey we experience a descent right before a glorious rise, we go into the dark to emerge out in the light. Usually accompanying a creative (or actual) birth is a rebirth for the one giving new life.

You do not need to experience childbirth to see the depth of your strength, there are many other types of moments in life that offer this reflection. What have those moments been for you?

One that comes to mind for me is the hike I did in Japan on the Kumano Kodo pilgrimage in 2016. There were very steep inclines, full days of hiking, some rough terrain, some rain. I was not physically prepared, every part of my body ached each night and even more so in the morning when it came time to rise early and do it all again. Something that gave me solace during that adventure was one of the people I was with telling me that "the mind gives up at only 10% of what the body can achieve." While I never fact checked this claim, it gave me great solace at the time to really trust that my body would make it through, and it did. It took my physical strength, and it also took a softness in my mind and heart to keep putting one foot in front of the other.

You are strong and soft, capable of what seems impossible, and full of depth.

Womb wisdom: summary

- Your creative animation begins with your first breath as you emerge from the womb.
- Your cervix is a sacred example of setting boundaries that serve you.
- The womb holds the space for union between the masculine and feminine, leading to all creation.
- Your womb governs your inner seasons of archetypes whose powers you get to harness through your cycles.
- Creation and beauty always emerge from darkness.
- Your relationship with your sexuality is the same relationship you have with your creativity.
- You are abundance incarnated, prosperity is meant for you, always.
- Your womb is the governing point for all pure emotions, these emotions serve as divine signals for your creative energy.
- The pulse of your clit is the pulse of your cosmic alignment.
- The way you irrationally destroy in a fit of rage is a sacred part of your creative story.
- Your ancestry holds much creative depth that you get to tap into, transcend, and creative art from.
- The divine parallel between physical life and creative life is present from the moment you start flirting back with the universe.
- You hold the depth of being strong and soft, always.

CHAPTER FIVE
THE JOURNEY THROUGH YOUR BODY

With one breath the light enters and floods, yet the light was already within. This is the beautiful paradox, be in your body to feel where to go and how to begin.

Sacred Symbolism – the jellyfish

The jellyfish is a creature that becomes one with the environment it is in. Being made up of 98% water, the jellyfish blends into the ocean. When the jellyfish washes up to the shore, within hours it becomes one with the wind, evaporating into the air. Wherever they find themselves, they are immersed, therefore nature becomes their guide.

The jellyfish has no bones, brain, lungs, or heart, it does have a nervous system which detects light and vibrations in the water. The jellyfish produce their own light, they are iridescent within the water. As the jellyfish lives its life in the waters of the oceans, it flows in solitary very rarely joining a group.

The jellyfish is a creature of flow, simplicity, and surrender.

There is at least one species of jellyfish that is seen as being immortal, for it constantly undergoes cellular trans-differentiation, being born from itself again and again. The jellyfish is mysterious to science, as it leaves no traces of itself behind, it makes it difficult for those driven by the mind and logic to understand it.

The life of the jellyfish gives us much to contemplate about the way we exist within nature, the way we move through different environments, and the way our light finds a home in our body. Creativity can move through our body as luminous light, and although we do not physically glow like the jellyfish, we energetically glow as the flow of life is radiant within us. When we allow creativity to move fully through our body, we allow an outward emanation of that inner light.

Much of this journey in allowing our inner light to flow through our body and emanate out is how willing we are to simplify the process of surrender. Are we willing to stop interfering with the natural environment we find ourselves in? Are we willing to be one with creation, so that we can express our differentiated genius?

Chakras are concentrated points of energy within your body; each chakra is like a wheel or spinning vortex of your vital life-force energy. There are 114 chakras within your body and higher bodies.

The primary seven chakras each govern aspects of our physical, mental, emotional, and spiritual vitality. As our creative ideas channel into and through our bodies, they take an energetic journey through our energy centres.

First landing in the crown, to the third eye, throat, heart, to the solar plexus, sacral and landing in the root.

This energetic journey is all about grounding the creative idea to the earth so that it can be materialised in our world. Coming in through our most spiritual centre, the crown, and landing in the root, our base grounding chakra.

When you allow your chakras to be open with a pure flow of energy you amplify the divine landscape that your creative ideas journey through within you. Amplifying the potency and transmission of the creation itself.

In this chapter we will explore the journey of creative ideas as they move through each of the primary chakras, along with insight into how each of these chakras play a role in your creative journey.

Crown – the divine channel

The little butterfly (your creative idea) flies into your field of awareness through the crown. This butterfly may have been playing around on earth for a little while already or the beacon of light emanating from your crown may have reached them in the far corners of the cosmos. The butterfly feels your light, your spiritual divineness, and your humanness, seeing you as the perfect being to bring them to life.

The little butterfly enters your crown and becomes flooded with light, they begin playing in your divine wisdom, in your direct channel to Source. Them being within this field opens new portals of potential for you to explore and play within.

In this space they feel no pressure, just potential. Pure lightness.

Your crown chakra is your direct link to Source, or God, or the Universe, whatever name you like to give divine oneness. I most often use Source. This link opens a new channel of divine wisdom and knowing, you sense your limitless potential here. Through this channel you call in light and wisdom from around the cosmos. There are light codes that only you can bring to Earth, and you get to infuse your creations, and your life, with these codes.

How receptive you are to this channelling of energy is largely influenced by your intention and your openness to life itself.

A sacred message the crown chakra holds is to love the experience of your life while embracing your spiritual essence.

Your value is in existing. There is nothing you *have* to do; you do not have to prove yourself to Source. Your purpose is to be you – you have nothing to defend and nothing to prove to anyone. You don't even have to help others, but you naturally do through your creative impulse. And that can be expressed in many ways.

Many butterflies will come and play in this space with you, sometimes their journey ends here and they leave your field.

If you allow them to stay, with the intention to bring them to life, they keep moving down your body.

Third Eye – the wonder of the worlds

In your crown the butterfly can *sense* the potential while being infused with your light. In the third eye the butterfly can *see* the potential and become infused with your vision.

In your imagination your little creative butterfly plays in the jungle gym of your mind, while also sharing their vision with you. This is where these two visions merge together to create clarity in how this idea will live in the world once it has completed its journey through you to be born in the world.

This chakra governs the energy of your imagination, and your spiritual intuition. It governs your capacity to see beyond the limits of your current reality and the limits of the collective worldview.

Your experience within your imagination is a creative and spiritual experience. Your imagination is a divine gift.

In this energy all things are instantly manifested, this means when ideas download into your awareness, you can bring them into this realm to play with the potential of different paths. You get to play with ideas and dance with them *before* they become more grounded and eventually birthed in the world. The material experience may not completely match your imagined one, but it will carry the same core essence that you connect with here.

The 64th Gene Key's gift is imagination which is channelled from its siddhi of illumination. Richard Rudd's transmission shares "to be illuminated by the 64th siddhi is to remain empty, while being constantly flooded with the rainbow colours of the inner aurora – it is to be an easel for the imagination of the universe itself."

Or as Osho says in his book Creativity, "imagination is the one faculty you have that comes closest to God."

This butterfly is a celestial being, an agent of Source, being used to metaphorically paint with the world as its canvas, through you. How you imagine painting the world within your third eye will heavily influence the path you choose to take in your material reality.

Throat – the activated voice

Here the butterfly becomes attuned to the tone and resonance of your voice. It is revealed to the butterfly what you are here to express, and the transmission your art and impact carries. The butterfly begins to vibrate in the rhythm of your expression.

Your throat chakra governs your voice, expression, and communication. This goes beyond what you say out loud, or what you write, you can communicate and express through your energy, body, and thoughts.

Your voice, the words you use and the tone in which you say them, holds a powerful frequency. Your voice is a powerful transmuter of energy.

Your voice will be incredibly activating for some, and maybe triggering for others. Your voice is *moving*, it is a force that impacts others.

When you bite your tongue, swallow your words, and hold yourself back from sharing what it is that you long to say – you dilute the potential and potency of your art's story.

Look at all the ways you have been holding your voice back from yourself, others, and the world.

There is often some wounding that arises when we begin to tune more deeply into the frequency of our own voice. Many people do not like the sound of their own voice. Often this is because when we hear ourselves speak we hear through our bones, but when we listen to a recording we hear through our ears. This can convince our mind that 'we don't really sound like that' when we hear recordings of ourselves. This is all just noise to move through.

Practise listening to your voice. Fall in love with your voice. All it takes is being willing to listen to it. Practise softness and love through the discomfort in the beginning. I promise the more you practise, the more comfortable it becomes.

If you have this fear around what your voice sounds like that stops you from speaking and using your voice in the way you feel called to, it can stagnant the flow within this energy centre. Thus, diluting the glow of the butterfly.

Your full expression is what allows the art to flow from your creative energy out into the world in the form it is meant to take. This is also what allows your creations to carry the transmission they are meant to. When the butterfly is born with the frequency of your activated voice it sends out a beacon to all those who are meant to find it.

The more you express, the more you play. The more you play, the more you refine. Your expression will expand when you allow yourself to play with it. Your art will be amplified in many ways as it continues to journey through your body.

Heart – the sacred bridge

The butterfly then lands in your heart, a peaceful and powerful place. Here it is in the holy ground between the limitless spiritual realm it has been playing in, and the grounded material world it longs to enter. In this sense your heart chakra is the bridge between the ethereal world and the material world. The butterfly transitions here from playing in the ethereal that they are so familiar with, and stepping into the material world to take a new form.

The heart chakra governs unconditional love, acceptance, peace, compassion, empathy. For feminine identifying beings, it is our portal for giving. In life we give through the heart and receive through the sacral.

Your heart chakra is also the home of your soul and inner child, it is a powerful portal as it is the bridge between your lower and higher chakras. Your lower chakras are grounded to your human/primal energy and your higher chakras are connected to your spiritual/divine self. The heart is what meets in the middle and holds all expressions of you.

Because of this it is likely that messages you want to share, causes you want to contribute to, experiences you want to explore, relationships you desire, are all a longing from your heart space.

Your heart is such a beautiful leader when it comes to making art out of life. Your heart will always guide you towards what is really important.

In making art out of your own life, this expression already impacts the world around you. Your expression already contributes to the evolution of the world.

The butterfly is connecting to all of this that glows within your heart, they again become infused with your energy.

The 4th Gene Key holds beautiful insights to the power of our heart chakra (which is the 4th primary chakra). The 4th Gene Key's siddhi of forgiveness is a "primary agent of Divine Grace… its ultimate role is to bring humanity into a collective union."

Richard Rudd goes on in his transmission to say that "forgiveness represents an involving force rather than an evolving force because it literally comes from the future towards that past." Here we see another layer of time not being linear, in your heart chakra your butterfly creative idea is imbued with this force, with the heart of the future.

In the gift frequency of this 4th Gene Key there is this ability that "leads you to a universal understanding of the rhythmic patterns and tendencies of life," which in turn "propels your awareness out of the mind." In this awareness there is true understanding that is felt through your whole body.

"When the 4th gift is freed from having to solve your existence, it finally comes into its real genius – to play with the patterns of existence and arrange them in new and original ways."

When your creative butterfly is immersed in this energy it begins to really see and feel the impact its presence will have in the world. While still playing with pure potential, it weaves this in with the material reality. The butterfly begins to understand. To understand its place in the world.

The butterfly crosses the bridge into your lower primal chakras to continue its journey through you into the world.

Solar Plexus – the confident power

Your butterfly lands in a more grounded place here, more connected to the material world than the previous steps in their journey thus far.

Here the butterfly becomes infused with a more material flavour of your purpose, and they feel the raw power you have within you. Here it is like they are within the glow of the sun, a fiery energy that is centred in its purpose.

Your solar plexus chakra governs your personal power, drive, ambition, and confidence. This is the centre that drives you to take action, in turn putting the energy of your creative ideas in motion to gain momentum.

In this part of the journey the butterfly meets your human power, which also opens space for some distortions of that power. There are two aspects of your power and confidence that we will explore here – your identity and decision making.

What we believe to be true about ourselves (our identity) and the decisions we make play a huge role in the action we take in bringing creative ideas to life, how we hold space for them in our body, and the form they take entering the world through us.

Identity

Our identity is formed by our identity statements, the background narrative our subconscious mind has about who we are and what we are capable of.

We often form these core statements in our most formative years up to seven years old. The child's mind accepts what it sees as truth without the capacity to apply rational thinking.

As adults we often have identity statements so deeply ingrained that actually originated from something external and never held any truth. But because we accepted it as truth at the time the statement was formed, it became our truth in the life we lived. Many decisions were then made because of these statements which continued to reinforce them, most of this playing out at a subconscious level.

In your early education you may have formed an inner statement like 'I am not good at maths.' Because your teacher outright told you this, or maybe your parents made a joke about it, or you deduced it because you got lower grades than your friends or compared to your other classes. If a teacher told you this, then that is much more of a reflection on them than it is you. If the 'low' grades were the external origins for this inner statement, your teacher may not have known how to cater for your learning style, the tests may have not been structured in the best way, there are many other reasons that do not necessarily mean that you were 'bad' at maths.

Could it be possible that the identity statement around being bad at maths was the source of the inner dialogue convincing you not to even attempt more creative problem solving for the maths questions, as opposed to the way you were being taught not making sense to your mind at the time?

How did that identity statement shape the experiences and opportunities you allowed yourself to pursue into adulthood?

Are there elements of your creativity you felt drawn to but because it involved something you told yourself you were 'bad' at so you didn't explore how it could be possible for you?

There was an experiment conducted in 1964 by a Harvard professor named Robert Rosenthal. He set out to explore what would happen to different students' test results if the teachers were told that certain kids were predisposed to succeed, and that other students were predisposed to not learn well.

He went into classrooms and gave the students a standard IQ test, telling the teacher it was a 'Harvard Test of Inflected Acquisition'. He told the teacher that the test would reveal which students had special abilities and would very likely experience a dramatic growth in their IQ.

After the test, Rosenthal chose several students from every class completely randomly. Even though there was nothing material to differentiate the student's IQ, he told the teachers that the students he selected were predicted to have that dramatic growth in their IQ.

All students were followed over a two-year period. The discovery of this experiment was that the teacher's expectations of these students had a significant effect on the students' learning.

He found that the teachers' expectations affected how the teacher's interacted with the different students in 'a thousand invisible ways.' If a student that the teacher expected to have a 'high IQ' didn't understand something, they took more time to help them, assuming that it was them themselves who needed to explain or help in a different way. If the teacher expected the student to have a 'low IQ' then when that student didn't understand something, the teacher assumed it was because of the student's low IQ.

Even though there was no baseline difference between all of these students, because of their teacher's expectations some students significantly outperformed others. This was only over a two-year period!

All of the teachers and other adult role models you had in your life as a child may have seemed like 'experts' when you were young, but remember now that they were just people. They had biases and unconscious narratives about all the students they taught.

To the child's mind, the world does revolve around them. If they witness something happening around them, it is internalised to mean that something about them caused it. This may be the truth at times, but the child's mind doesn't have the capacity to think through what other variables may have been involved in the given situation, or the emotional maturity to process some events.

When it comes to everything you think you know to be true about yourself – be curious and prepared to discover that some things you have taken as a given fact may not actually be true at all.

Maybe with more self-sourced confidence and encouragement, and the right support, you could do anything that you have told yourself isn't possible for you. – including being creative-af and bringing amazing, big, and meaningful creative ideas to life in the most effortless and amazing way.

There are many identity statements within you. Some have been very serving to the adventure and art of your life, and some have been limiting your creativity and life. Be open and curious as you revisit the statements that you want to reframe, to reclaim a part of yourself you have hidden without giving it a real chance to play.

Decisions

Your decisions and how you follow through is a testament to your confidence and your trust in life.

Your decisions are what put you in motion. Being in motion is what allows you to gain momentum.

The truth about decisions is that you can't get it wrong. There is no such thing as good or bad, right or wrong. You impose the meaning, and you impose any morality. To be in your power, choose to believe that every decision you make IS the right decision for that moment. This way you don't allow energy leaks from continuous doubt. Thoughts of doubt and fear are natural parts of being human but you don't actually have to engage with these thoughts – laugh them off, tell them to fuck off, throw them a going away party. But don't perpetually spiral with them.

You made the right decision. You will make the right next decision.

Keep putting yourself in motion and trust that the momentum WILL catch up with you. In the meantime, you get to enjoy the journey.

Remember that these creative butterflies chose *you* to bring them to life. The butterfly becomes infused with your confidence here, it trusts in your decision making.

Sacral – the sensual sea

When the butterfly lands in your sacral it gets to swim in the full sweetness of your creative juices. Here it swims through your inner oceans of abundance, the depth of your pure emotions, and full depth of wherever your inner waters contain.

The butterfly becomes infused with your radiant life-force, your creative energy, and it completes its divine channelling into your body. The divine codes, and spiritual essence of the butterfly is fully incarnated in your sacral, as it is on the cusp of entering the world. The butterfly is floating, swimming, dancing, flowing. Embracing these final moments of complete safety and unity with you. There is full trust in you putting everything in place for its arrival in the world. There is surrender to whatever shall unfold next.

Your sacral chakra is the energy centre in your lower abdominal, or your womb space. We have already explored some of its depth throughout Chapter Four. This chakra governs your emotions, abundance, creative energy, sensuality, sexuality, and feminine energy.

This chakra is all about the juice of being alive, and being human. When you let the sweet waters within you flow freely, this soft ease is mirrored outwards through your life. There may be moments when you panic or doubt yourself and try to control the waters, or you try to force yourself against the natural flowing currents. There is so much ease and liberation in allowing the currents to take you where they will, imagine paddling upstream and the full body relief when you allow yourself to be in the moment and allow yourself to be taken with the flow.

Root – the grounded foundation

The butterfly moves through its final portal as it is birthed into the world and takes its material form. Moving through this portal of your root chakra, it becomes grounded to our earth. From this moment the butterfly has a life of its own, while connected to you, the life is sovereign and separate from you. The butterfly begins to form their own identity out in the world, one that you help shape, but one that you do not control.

Your root chakra governs your sense of safety and survival. When you feel safe and secure, you can play in your creator mode with ease. This chakra is deeply connected to the earth, being with nature helps to activate the feeling of groundedness that balances your sense of safety.

When in survival mode, the fight to survive consumes you. This has ensured our survival throughout history. Where this can interfere with our creativity now is when there is no actual threat, but our fear convinces us that there is. The body doesn't feel safe to create in these circumstances. Your body won't let you bring your most beautiful creations into the world until it feels safe to rest into the process.

Even though this is the final chakra the butterfly moves through within your body to be born on earth, how grounded and balanced this chakra is influences how safe your body feels to allow the butterfly to enter your energy at all.

As the butterfly moves through your body, it interacts and immerses in all of your energy.

Each of your chakras could be distorted in some way, over-active, under-active, closed, some drawing energy from another – these imbalances within your energy system can lead to a distorted journey for the butterfly. Your creative ideas can then take form in the world that holds the transmission of these distortions. Some will be very subtle, and some will be abruptly destructive.

The butterfly will always touch your highest frequency energy as well. The more radiant you allow yourself to be, the more radiant a journey your butterfly will have.

Everything is all in divine timing, you will learn many lessons through the journey that each butterfly takes through you, once it has been born in the world.

The journey through your body: summary

- Each of our seven primary chakras holds holy ground for our creative ideas to journey through within our body, preparing the creative idea to enter the material world through us.
- Crown – the creative idea enters your field of awareness and becomes flooded with your divine light.
- Third eye – the creative idea plays within the potential of your imagination exploring the possibilities for its life on earth.
- Throat – the creative idea tunes to the resonance of your voice.
- Heart – the creative idea crosses the bridge from the divine to the primal while swimming in the power of your love.
- Solar plexus – the creative idea becomes infused with your purpose and mission to begin grounding its own earthly purpose.
- Sacral – the creative idea becomes imbued with your radiant life-force as it completes its channelling into your physical body.
- Root – the creative idea is birthed into the world becoming grounded to the earth.

CHAPTER SIX
THE DEPTHS OF BEING HUMAN

Arrive at the temple of your flesh and bones, swim in the red sea of blood. Feel your depths as you open your eyes, embrace yourself as your temple floods.

Sacred Symbolism – the serpent

The serpent has a polarising force in the world. For some it is seen as a symbol for transformation and renewal, for others a symbol to be feared.

In religious stories about the garden of Eden, it was the serpent who encouraged Eve to eat the apple, the forbidden fruit. Labelled as a conniving and deceptive trickster, the serpent was seen as evil. The symbol of Ouroboros, the serpent that eats its own tail continually, has also been labelled as 'evil.' In both of these examples there is light within and the distorted labels are a projection of human fears.

If Eve and Adam were not meant to eat the apple, why did God, or The Creator, place it there? If it weren't for the apple then they would never have had the full human experience that they got to live. Ouroboros is a symbol for the eternal cycles of creation and destruction, the serpent continually devours itself, and simultaneously is born again. This is our human experience, life is always beginning and ending. In this sense the serpent represented in this way is a symbol for unity, life could not exist without death, and death could not exist without life. Creation could not exist without destruction; it is a natural cycle.

As the serpent grows it sheds its skin frequently, as it moves through its life into maturity it continues to shed but only two or three times a year. Each time the serpent sheds, it leaves behind its own skin to reveal the new scales that have been forming underneath. You too shed your skin as you grow and evolve. While the serpent relies on an external heat source, being solar powered, it is adaptable, able to survive a year without eating if it must.

The serpent is dynamic in its existence and in how others perceive it, just like you as a human. The serpent represents the primal life-force moving through your body, connected to the full depth of being human.

The spectrum of being human

We live in a world of polarity, where whatever exists through creation simultaneously births its polar opposite. Yin and yang, feminine and masculine, rich and poor, night and day, dark and light, and so on. The polarity creates a spectrum from which we get to experience life within. This polarity and spectrum that exists in the world is reflected within, and from, our inner world. The microcosm of our body is a mirror to the macrocosm of the universe.

As Carolyn Elliott puts it in her book Existential Kink, "as humans, our whole selves are always reflections of the divine totality. We are microcosmic reflections of the total holy macrocosm, and as such, we are each innately curious about and desirous for the full spectrum of potential experience, both the painful and the pleasurable, the evil and the good, the ugly and the beautiful."

Part of our human story is to unlock our inner gifts, by moving through the challenges of our shadows. This is a core element to the path of The Gene Keys. The polarity that exists in the gene keys is the shadow and the gift, with the third frequency band, the siddhi, being the divine essence, or the seed to both. The shadow and the siddhi could also be seen as polar opposites that create a spectrum in which the gift sits. In whatever way we explore it, as humans we all have a unique sequence of shadows to live through that allow us to gain more inner depth and to fully unlock the gifts that we were born with within our DNA.

As I quoted earlier in the book, in the transmission for the 28th Gene Key, Richard Rudd says "we are each born with a creative purpose that no other human being carries. If you are to release your true creativity into the world, you must meet your own dark side."

In other words, we must face our shadows in order to fully experience our gifts and our full creative expression. Our gifts give us each a personalised flavour of creativity that we get to share in the world. When we embrace our human gifts we can always use them in service to the whole of humanity.

Part of being human is embracing how messy life can be, when we embrace the mess, mundane, magic, madness, and all within life in its totality, we allow ourselves to live within the full spectrum.

In Existential Kink, Carolyn Elliot explores the kinky way to do shadow work, she states "when you integrate your shadow, you become much more capable of receiving big beauty and big bounty in your life because you're no longer accidentally unknowingly rejecting it. This is magic."

In embracing the full spectrum, you realise that the mundane *is* magic, and that magic *is* mundane.

Our human experience is pretty freaking magical when you pause in reverence to all the things that happen in our body and in our world. In the integration of what appears to be opposite we can access a new layer of depth where we meet them in crossover, not in neutral inertia but in full union. Like the infinity symbol they have a point of merging together before space is created to go to their own polar side once more, and again and again.

Your creative potential lies within how deeply you embrace your human-ness. It can be tempting to only play within the higher realms, and your spiritual practices may at times lead you away from your human-ness, but know that your creative power is in your body, and the depth of that power will be found in how you play with life within yourself.

Emotions and their influence on your creative expression

Emotions are (e)nergy in motion. Through our emotions a charge is generated in our body, depending on the frequency of the charge, we experience different sensations and feelings. Our emotions can lead to certain thoughts and behaviours, and conversely, our thoughts and behaviours can lead to certain emotions arising.

Because of the charge our emotions produce within our body, they can be used creativity to access more of our own depth, and to make art with.

Some emotional charges engender destructive expressions of our creativity, those same emotional charges can be alchemised within us to create some of our most beautiful art.

In this section we will explore some of the main emotional charges that become interwoven with our creative expression.

FEAR

If there is one sneaky sensation that will always try to sabotage you, its name would be fear.

Fear takes its role in your body very seriously, its primary role is to keep you safe. Fear can do a good job at this when it convinces you to not jump off a cliff, or eat a poison berry, things that your naïve curiosity could convince you to do just to see what it is like if fear wasn't around (the image of my nephew trying to take a step off a huge ledge, or my niece putting just anything in her mouth, come to mind. Children are not born with fear and innately are curious to experience everything). The irony is that fear takes its role too seriously. It sees the way to keeping you safe, as keeping you exactly as you are, that means any kind of creative expression (that will always be expansive) will often be viewed as unsafe to the fear in your body.

This feeling can stem from many places within your psyche, always being linked to the ultimate human fear of your nonexistence, fear cannot accept the fact of death and it takes futile measures to try to gain some level of control. In trying to control the 'bad' staying away, the grip becomes too tight, and your creative expression suffers.

Fear will divert your attention away from your creative impulse when it has weaselled its way into control. At one point fear gained a larger presence within you compared to your creativity, your intuition, and love. It doesn't matter how this happened, now by bringing your awareness to how fear has been sneakily influencing you, you can shift your relationship with this feeling.

Elizabeth Gilbert, author of Big Magic, says "your fear will always be triggered by your creativity, because creativity asks you to enter into realms of uncertain outcome, and fear hates uncertain outcome." In Elizabeth Gilbert's definition of creative living, she says she is referring to "living a life that is driven more strongly by curiosity than by fear."

Julia Cameron, author of The Artist Way, says that artists who are blocked are often called 'lazy' but that we should call it what it is – fear. She says that "the cure is love."

Merging both of these paths for curing the influence fear has had on your creativity, following both your curiosity and love, can be healing to the effect fear has had on you , and also an artistic journey in and of itself.

When you are curious about your fear and allow said fear to be softened by your love, you see it's true intention – to keep you safe. You also see that your fear is coming from a child version of yourself, at a time when you learnt to fear. This child, while an important part of you, should not be in charge of making decisions about your creativity or big elements of your life. Can the more mature, embodied part of you take back this responsibility of decision making?

In your curiosity and love, the fear naturally transcends its heaviness and transforms into excitement. Excitement is an amazing fuel for your creative action.

SHAME

In Brené Brown's exploration into The Power of Vulnerability, she differentiates shame from embarrassment. In moments that we feel embarrassed we can recognise that the joke is in our actions, the embarrassment is temporary and eventually laughed off. Shame however is when the same event could occur, but we internalise the experience to mean that *we* are the joke, there is something wrong with us. Shame can be paralysing and keeps the focus on us being the problem.

Shame can have a heartbreaking influence on your creative expression and the art that you feel safe to share with the world. When you are under the (false) impression that there is something wrong with you, this inevitably leads to (also false) impression that there is always something wrong with your art. So much so that you feel ashamed of whatever you create.

If left unchecked, shame can suffocate your creativity and

original expression. As shame drives you to believe that something is wrong with you it can drive you to pretend to be somebody else, making all that you express inauthentic to your true artistry.

Carolyn Elliott shares in Existential Kink that "a significant number of folks find it necessary to numb and hide this sense of wrongness by using every available form of addiction." And then advises "let's transmute that feeling of "wrongness" into raw, hot, glorious power."

Brené Brown shares that the antidote to shame is empathy.

I believe in taking both approaches, to give great empathy to myself while any feeling of shame or wrongness about myself arises in my body, and then transmute it into that hot glorious power!

Shame can drive destructively negative self-talk in a way that paints a dimly lit false image of who you really are, and of what you create.

To begin healing your shame, you must allow yourself to feel it. Once you do touch this place inside of you, you can take that perverted charge and turn it in on itself. Make your shame feel shameful about itself. This can sound counterproductive, as the saying goes, two wrongs don't make a right, but two negatives multiplied do make a positive, it is all about the perspective you choose to take.

Once your shame feels shamed, it will feel ashamed for ever making you feel a drop of shame. This is the opening for deeper empathy for yourself, and for others who have ever felt the same shame.

Healing your shame and arriving at a place where you really let it dawn on you that there was never anything wrong with you, will unleash a tidal wave of your creative energy that your shame was holding back. This allows you to create with more freedom, letting your authentic artistry shine through your life. Look at where your shame has been diluting your art, and be willing to admit that you were wrong about anything being wrong about you.

ANGER

Your anger could be the fire that completely revives your creativity. Anger is an interesting emotion to explore as the experience and perception of anger is wildly different for different people.

For women and predominantly feminine people, when anger is expressed or even hinted at, they are painted as highly irrational and chaotic. It isn't acceptable within our society.

For men and predominantly masculine people, anger has somehow been rebranded as not being an emotion. Anger is seen as passion and care, sometimes as violence.

In this section I am going to explore anger as a raw emotion and I encourage you to navigate the relationship that you have with your own anger. I am going to mainly speak to those who feel their anger buried. For those with buried anger, you likely do not feel safe to fully express your anger in a way that allows space for change.

Your anger is always arising with a purpose, to drive some kind of change. As Julia Cameron says "anger points the way, not just the finger."

When it comes to your creativity, there may be periods of your life where you feel it is buried under the fog of inertia, like the fire is out and you don't even know how to begin to reignite it. Even when the fire isn't roaring, there are always embers burning, your creative fire can never be completely put out. To fan the flames and get that fire going again, first you need to break through the fog. To do that – GET ANGRY.

Anger is a gift that can help you clear the way, uphold your boundaries, and tune in with your passionate spark.

To move through your anger you have to be willing to feel it, feeling your anger doesn't mean that you have to erupt hot lava all over anyone in close proximity. You can use the explosion of anger in a healthy way. Let your anger help you get shit done.

When the fire burns through the fog your creative fire will be burning more brightly and will drive you into productive action.

Bring awareness to feeling the heat in your body and be mindful of where and how you direct it.

Fire as an element brings non-reversible change, once something has gone up in flames it cannot return to its original state, this is the force of your power. As Uncle Ben said to Peter Parker (AKA Spiderman) "with great power comes great responsibility."

FRUSTRATION

As we follow our creative impulses and pursue our creative dreams, we will invariably come across bumps in the road, re-directions, and dead-ends. There will be some projects that were just not meant to come to life for you, or that didn't meet the timeline you hoped for. When we look at the big picture of our entire life we can see that each of these bumps were tiny and that they all resulted in us going exactly where we needed to go. In the moment however, they can feel really big.

We do not need to bypass the disappointment and frustration we will likely feel in moments of our creative journey, feel it in your body and don't let it mean anything about who you are or the value of your art. We do not need to bypass the feeling, and we also do not need to dwell in it either.

Elizabeth Gilbert says that "learning how to endure your disappointment and frustration is part of the job of a creative person."

There are many different paths to enduring the disappointments and frustrations that are part of the journey, some practices are – reminding yourself of the bigger picture, giving yourself a set limit to scream or cry about it (whether that is one minute or one hour), writing a breakup letter to these feelings then burning it, or any other method that feels like a clean release for you.

This is part of the journey when you care about what you are creating – this is a good thing. Your creative life is so much bigger than these little set back moments and the feelings they may produce.

JEALOUSY

Our minds are wired to measure by comparison. We know that something is big by knowing that something else is small in comparison. We know that others are successful by knowing what average and unsuccessful looks like. This wired comparison can set us up for jealousy.

When we see those who have the relationships, money, love, success, family, attention, anything else that we want, and that we don't currently have, jealousy can generate inside of us.

Once the emotion has hit the body, the signal this energy sends can trigger various reactions. You could get angry at yourself for being jealous, you could feel guilty for not being more happy for the other person, you could feel shame for having such a 'terrible' emotion come up for you. There are many ways that jealousy can make you spiral into other thoughts and feelings. Ultimately stemming from the thought – I have less than I want. Or some variation of that focused on something you want to have, or something you want to be more like.

This can have a number of influences over your creativity, mainly driving you to believe that you do not have enough to create like other people. Whether physical resources or personal talent, they have something that you do not possess.

When we take the feeling of jealousy as a signal to turn inwards it can be incredibly revealing to our desires. We can sort through what is at the core of what the other person has that we want. Our jealousy can then be alchemised into inspiration and resourcefulness.

When you ground your clear desire, and you are willing to explore what you are jealous of, you can also explore how that could be possible for you too. You can transcend all of your jealousy into inspiration and resourcefulness as fuel to get what you really want and create the art you desire to. Throughout your creative journey you will find that there are some core desires that you can only give yourself, like love, reverence, autonomy, and there are desires that you can allow to come to life for you in a way that aligns with your creative energy.

I have mainly focused on lower frequency emotions in this section as within those emotions lies the charge of huge creative power when they are felt and alchemised in the body, and because they are some of the biggest ways our creative expression can become perverted and destructive, or stagnant and dry.

Your higher frequency emotions can of course offer beautiful and illuminating energy for your creativity and your art. It is our higher frequency emotions like excitement, love, joy, and peace that naturally align with our creative impulse. When we are in higher frequency states we naturally move with the universal flow of creation, we feel more intuitive, and are more creative within ourselves. Play with what emotion you love to create with. For me I have very natural excitement and it is a beautiful fuel in many of my creative pieces. What higher frequency emotions come most naturally to you? How do you best support yourself to touch in with that emotion?

Love is your natural state, the more you connect with love the more creative you will feel. The more creative you feel, the more you will connect with that feeling of love.

Your emotions are incredibly powerful, all of them. They are signals, portals, and energy that you get to use in your creative expression in different ways.

How your pain can fuel your art

The pain that you experience in your life is expansive for your art.

It draws you down into the depths of your being, it pulls you apart then leaves you to piece yourself back together. Your pain can feel unbearable, yet you bore it and you are still here. Your pain forces you inwards. Your pain can be triggered by many sources, both external and internal.

What your pain cannot do is change who you fundamentally are at your core, it cannot change the creative essence of your being. Your experiences may change the surface expression of you, but never the core inner light that is always emanating through you.

What your pain can do, is provide more contrast and energy from which you can draw on creatively and make art with.

The challenges your pain creates prompt you to grow, and to meet more of yourself in the process.

There is a quote I love by Cesar A. Cruz "art should comfort the disturbed and disturb the comfortable."

Your pain is relatable, those disturbed by that same pain will relate deeply to the art that you create from it. And those comfortable in the realm of your pain will be disturbed enough to consider a new perspective. They may even be disturbed enough so that it shatters their judgements towards others and opens more compassion and empathy inside of them.

Some will hide from this disturbance in their comfort and that is ok, you do not need to comfort them through their discomfort of being disturbed by what you create.

People will always apply their own meaning and your art will take on a life of its own, creating many moments of inner reflection that has an ever-lasting flow on affect in how it plays out in the lives of others.

The pain in your body can lead your creative energy to invent a product or service that deeply helps others in your situation, or to simply give comfort and the feeling that they are not alone.

The grief that you sink into can be your most potent reminder for how precious your life is and open you to pour your heart into living fully, your greatest art project.

Your crippling jealousy could lead to an entertaining drama filled romantic comedy screenplay, that potentially gets turned into a movie, or maybe it is something you act out in your living room while intoxicated with your friends.

Your sadness can lead to the most heart-breaking song that helps others heal their sadness by feeling that someone finally put to words what they were feeling.

Olivia Rodrigo's album Sour was written from the perspective of a bitter (her word) 17-year-old about heartbreak, betrayal, and relationship conflict. Millions of people around the world deeply resonated to the painful emotions that she was drawing from. Listening to Sour felt extremely cathartic and healing for my inner 17-year-old-self.

In 2021 I wrote my first poetry book, Wander, which was a compilation of my inner thoughts about some heavy emotions I was carrying, told through rhyming verses. Making this piece of art through my own pain was very healing, and so many people told me how my poems helped them tap in deeper with their own emotions.

When we put words, or images, or any kind of artful expression to the pain we feel inside, we harness the pain creativity. This is an alchemising and healing experience for us, and potentially for many others. We do not always have to share the art that comes from our pain, sometimes it can be just for us. When you feel called to share it, it is always powerful.

Take a moment to sit in a safe space with your pain, take a moment to breathe deeply into your body, pinpoint where the pain is inside of you and give it a voice. If your pain had this voice, what would it say to you? What would it have to say to the world?

Maybe it would just scream, laugh, or cry, and what a beautiful expressive moment of emotional art that would be.

Maybe you will feel an urge to pull out pen and paper, or the notes app on your phone, and your fingers will start writing.

Maybe your body will be called to dance, shake, or jump.

Whatever pours out is art.

It could be a moment of art. Or it could be the basis of something you come back to when the charge of your pain has subsided, and you have the space to refine it while maintaining its artistic integrity.

I do not wish pain onto you, or anyone else. You will invariably experience moments of pain, as it is the nature of being human. We can alchemise our pain to use it as fuel in our creative expression. We can bring out beauty from within the darkness.

With the creative embrace of pain, we open ourselves to the depth we can feel within the spectrum of life. As is the law of polarity, the greater the pain the greater the potential for pleasure. As you tenderly embrace your pain, you embrace the totality of life, and with that your art naturally gains depth and power.

The embodiment of your depth

The full depth of your being can only be experienced through your body. Here on earth, your full creative depth can only pour out through, you guessed it, your body.

So many of us who were raised to believe we were not creative were also conditioned to live life through our minds. Our minds are extremely powerful, and we can lead us into some pretty awesome experiences living with this style of inner leadership. However, there will be a time for reckoning, where the body is finally screaming out for the attention you have deprived it of up until that point. Your body knows what it is doing and if your mind doesn't yield its fight for control, your body will find a way to humble your mind by shattering its illusion of control.

This humbling will be the moment your mind is shaken into questioning your entire reality and existence, it will question the control it always thought it had. This is good, lean into those existential questions as they will inevitably lead you back into your body.

In your body there is harmony, life-force, depth, and your full creative power.

Your body is far more powerful than your mind, but it doesn't deny the power of the mind.

The subconscious mind controls 95% of our thoughts, actions, behaviours, and everything that then ripples on. This is something that Dr Joe Dispenza has explored in his research, along with many others. The subconscious mind IS the body, and our body *is* our subconscious mind.

When we bring our energy back into our body, from our

mental space, we become extremely more present, intuitive, and creative.

In the embodiment of your depth there is integration between all parts of you. All parts recognised for their power and value to the whole of who you are.

In this integration there is synergy between your primal self and your divine self, where one plus one equals one thousand.

Meet yourself at the surface and be willing to travel inwards. You will meet many layers of yourself, some that may appear contradicting to the last. Let yourself be a hypocrite and walking-contradiction as you explore. There are worlds and worlds within you, and you need to be willing to look inwards to cultivate the innate depth you have within and allow it to glow through your body to the surface.

Once you meet any facet of your depth you can ground it in your body and embody it in your life. This *is* the art of living.

How your depth informs your art

The deeper you dive into your own depth, the more deeply you meet yourself. At your core is your essence. As you have been conditioned through life and your imprinted shadows emerge, fog and clouds can dull the outward shine of that light. But just like the sun is always shining regardless of the clouds, so too is your inner light. The light of the sun will always emanate through the fog and clouds – it is just that strong.

Moving through these layers within you opens you to more of your own depth. Moving through each layer opens a deeper understanding of life itself in your mind and body. The more layers of your inner world that you move through the more of your own innate wisdom you come into contact with.

Some people will remain on the surface their entire lives, unwilling to look at what truly lies within them. If you have been drawn to a book like this then I would say you are certainly not one of those people. There can be times that it feels challenging to have relationships or even conversations with those who lack a connection to their own depth, but it is not our place to judge the path that others are on, and we can never truly know the inner world that they experience. When you understand more of yourself you will naturally have a deeper understanding of others. Use this understanding to give them grace when needed, and always kindness.

Your art is an expression of your depth in the moment you create it. As you continue to evolve so too will the depth of your art.

You may look back on your works of art in a few years time and they may appear to be more surface level than the new creations being birthed from your being.

Within your exploration of your inner world, you will meet some of the polarising forces that I spoke of at the beginning of this chapter within yourself.

Let the conflict and contradictions exist, the friction between them makes way for the creation of art to come into the world through you. In the moment you make art there is union between the two poles, like the orgasm where they finally come together, until the forces part ways again and this cycle continues.

The depth of your inner world informs your art by allowing you to express reflections of your inner world outwards, and in the way it shapes your current perspective on the world, informing you where to pour your energy and art.

The more you live your beautiful human life, embracing all that comes with it, the more of your depth you will experience. It is all within you already.

The depths of being human: summary

- We live in a world of polarity, the very energy that makes creation possible. Across the spectrum of polarity, we experience the totality of life. To embrace the pleasure, we must too embrace the pain. To unleash our full creativity, we must too face our darkest fears.

- The energy of our emotions easily becomes entangled with our creative expression. Each emotion is a portal into a deeper sense of yourself, and more juicy creative energy to pour into your art.

  Fear can be a portal into excitement.

  Shame can be a portal into deep empathy and your authentic artistry.

  Anger can be a portal into passion and stronger boundaries.

  Frustration can be a portal into a wider view of your creative journey.

  Jealousy can be a portal into inspiration and resourcefulness.

- When you embrace your pain, you transcend it into art.

- Journeying inwards to your own depth allows you to swim in the full reservoir of your creative essence.

- Connecting with your own depth paves the way for your greatest art to flow into the world.

CHAPTER SEVEN
LIBERATION THROUGH CREATION

The day will arrive for you to thrive, for your heart to open and loving words to be spoken. To liberate your wings, your life of freedom soon begins. Fly, fly, far and high.

Sacred Symbolism – the dragonfly

The life cycle of the dragonfly begins in the egg that hatches into larva, and then undergoes a metamorphosis to be reborn as the dragonfly. As a larva, the dragonfly lives within the water, needing clean water to survive. Most of its life is spent in the water. Until the day comes for a transformation that is both sudden and a long time coming. The preparation can take several days, while the emergence takes mere hours for the larva to be completely transformed.

Unlike the butterfly who has to completely dissolve into itself before it can form again, the larva simply expands to shed its old form and stretch into the dragonfly.

While in the emergence, the dragonfly breathes in air for the first time, embracing this element. Then the dragonfly takes flight and quickly becomes a master of the air. There is lightness in this liberation. There is spaciousness and there is freedom.

The dragonfly is a sacred symbol of maturity, it was simply when this creature became mature enough it was liberated from the confines of the water and was able to fly in the spacious sky. It transcended its old conditioning. This is something that was an inevitable part of the story, yet a moment that could not be forced or rushed to. The dragonfly is a symbol for change, for growth, for liberation, and new beginnings.

Through the dragonfly's liberated chapter in its story, its wings are iridescent, they show different colours in different lights. A symbol of its multi-dimensional nature that is also an innate part of your liberation. Different lighting will reveal different colours of your essence, drawing on fragments of all that has been alchemised in your journey up to this point.

The dragonfly stays near fresh water as it only lives for mere weeks, it takes in life fully, seeks a mate and proceeds to lay its eggs, beginning this story of evolution and liberation once more.

Liberation is provoking you

Your creative energy yearns to be liberated, to be set free and allowed to be expressed in the world in all the magical ways you are capable and destined to make your art.

The essence of liberation is already within you, poking you and provoking you to wake up and see what is really important within your life. To see what is important in life itself.

When we let the pokes feel like playful tickles from life we can have fun with how we play through the challenges life presents in order for us to feel more free. These challenges may be to accept 'darker' parts of ourselves and allow them to be integrated into the whole of who we are, or ending and grieving relationships where the story has come to an end, or facing the mistakes we made that shook our financial stability, or the many other challenges that can come up in our life. All of which give us an opportunity to question who we will be as we move through them, what is important to us, and what needs to be refined in our life.

In the transmission for the 39th Gene Key, where liberation is the siddhi, Richard Rudd says that "liberation is a provocative energy – it tests and challenges those who are drawn to it." It is "the energy of liberation (that) ultimately provokes the realisation of freedom."

Liberation reaches out into life and provokes us through different challenges that can feel annoying and burdensome. Beneath the surface level annoyance we will find something deeper, a more raw emotion perhaps, that we can harness creatively to bring more freedom into our lives.

What is it that you yearn to be liberated from?

What heaviness has been attached to you for so long that you have forgotten the lightness you could experience once you liberate yourself?

Imagine yourself with wings, with a heavy weight attached to your ankle with a chain. There is a certain distance you can freely go but anything beyond that, as you reach the chain's limit, feels extremely hard to keep moving. With all your might you can lift the weight up to go a little higher but it will eventually pull you down as you feel exhausted and fatigued. When you finally liberate yourself from the chains, as you detach from the heaviness, you feel light, free, liberated.

As you let the force of liberation free you, you become a provocative force in the world. When others witness you freely flying it may provoke something within them, it is up to them whether they stay attached to their own heaviness or they use the provocation you have triggered to free themselves.

You being liberated is a powerful force in the world. Do not be afraid to be provocative, to fly higher than those around you. This does not place you above anyone else in value as a human being, it is about questioning how you really want to live your life. In your liberation your creativity has more freedom than ever before. If there were no limits to how you could paint the world, what colour and brush would you start with? If you were liberated from all limitations what would be the highest ideals that you would stand for? What would you live for? What would you create for?

Playing with these visionary prompts *now* tunes you into the higher purpose of your creativity – to be of service in the world while you playfully enjoy it. Your highest purpose is to be yourself, in which the purpose of your creativity naturally flows out of.

Liberate yourself from your past work

Sometimes art grows on you, sometimes you outgrow pieces of your art, none of this takes away from its intrinsic value as being part of the collective cosmic storyline of creation.

Whether you view your past work as proof that you peaked early and never reached the same level again, or on the other end of the spectrum that everything you have previously created is a disaster – it is time to liberate yourself from the confines of your past work. In liberating yourself from your past work you give yourself the space to soften into the present moment, where there isn't the heaviness of pressure, where your art isn't being compared to anything, where you allow what wants to be expressed to flow out.

I used to live in this paradox of wanting to be 'my best' *and* being afraid of being my best. Wanting to be my best to prove that I was worthy and to be recognised. And afraid to be my best because then it meant I would create a new standard that everyone would expect of me and that I couldn't possibly hit every time. This also applied to everything that I created. I would strive for greatness while simultaneously holding myself back. I fell into a mindset that nothing would be as good as what I had already done, I would never be able to top my previous efforts, while also knowing I was capable of more. This inner conflict stifled my creativity because I was living in my mind fantasising about the past and the future, leaving no time for the present moment throughout my daily life.

When you liberate yourself from your past work, and also liberate yourself from the attachment of what your future work needs to look like, you arrive in the present moment where you actually make your best art.

By your best art, I mean the best art for that moment that you are in. Here you do not feel the need to compare your art while you are channelling and creating it.

So what if others see you as a 'one hit wonder'?

So what if others see you as lost potential?

You are writing the narrative of your inner script.

You do not have to live up to your potential (that other people make up about you).

You do not need to live up to the artistry of your past work.

You have nothing to prove with your art.

If you created one beautiful drawing as a child and in turn every adult convinced you that you would be a great artist, but that didn't exactly pan out as you became an adult – let that shit go. Your artistry could have been poured into anything else.

When we were children, many adults loved asking 'do you know what you want to be when you grow up?' Of course, the answer they were looking for was a job title. If we gave an answer or showed any natural talent that fit what the adults thought would make us 'good' at a certain job, often they would hold us to that in their mind.

Since being around kids myself, sometimes I do find myself wondering who they will grow into, what work they may do, and what art they may create. Sometimes I catch myself about to ask the question - what do you want to be when you grow up? But I have such awareness of that projection of my own curiosity now that I always pause to consider what the better question is in that moment. It is always one that focuses on their joy and art now.

Some children do have an inner sense of what they will be doing in the world as adults and they live out their childhood dream, but most times these are just childhood dreams. Liberate yourself from the conditioned dreams you had as a child, liberate yourself from how others thought you would turn out based on the toys you liked to play with in your past.

There may come a time where you evolve completely past your previous work, you may have been well known in your inner circle, community, or wider audience for doing a certain thing, creating in a certain way, and then you feel the call that it is time to create and live in a new way. Liberating yourself from this past work at times requires you to liberate yourself from your old identity and from what you think others will think about your big change.

As someone who loves change, I have pivoted and made big adjustments in what I pour my life-force and creativity into many times. Sometimes that means making my past work unavailable going forward, sometimes it means letting that previous work keep circulating in the world and letting it have a complete life of its own, and sometimes it means taking pieces from what I was previously doing to integrate into my new vision. In any case there is a liberation from holding on for the sake of holding on to something that was already established.

There are many ways you may feel called to liberate yourself from your previous work, especially when you feel it keeping your mind and energy stuck in the past. Let yourself be liberated, let yourself be present to the moment you are living.

Liberate yourself from the dreams of others

The dreams of other people can be a persistent presence in our life that redirects our creative energy in ways that do not serve our true artistry or desires in life.

It could be the unfulfilled dreams of your parents being pushed onto you, and it could also be the collective dreams of society that you do not personally align with. If you feel pressure to fulfil these creative dreams on behalf of your parents or society, a big list of 'shoulds' become imprinted in the mind.

Osho says that "when a man (or woman/human) lives with thousands of should and should nots, he (she/they) cannot be creative.' While Julia Cameron believes that "often, creativity is blocked by our falling in with what other people's plan for us."

Take a moment of reflection for how the dreams of others have limited you creatively. What pressure and heaviness has this added that is diluting the potency of your creative expression?

One of the biggest ways that all these shoulds and pressures stifle your creativity is by driving you to only think logically, trying to plan our every detail of what you will create, how, when, and what exactly it will look like. This detailed plan gets in the way of creation moving through you to make beautiful art that carries the essence of you. As Osho also says, "logic is dry, poetry is alive." Your art is naturally juicy and poetic when it has the space to pour out of you.

It is time to pour all your juices into what you feel called to create, where your creative impulse is guiding you.

If you have been lost in the dreams of others for a long period of time it can feel a little like a maze to get out and back to the core of what you are really here to create yourself. The light at your core is always shining, guiding you back to yourself, follow the light, follow your bliss, one step at a time.

What will you create today that solely aligns with your dreams?

What 'shoulds' are you ready to dissolve?

Now is the time to liberate yourself from -

The dreams of your parents.

The dreams of society.

The dreams of your friends.

The dreams of your favourite fictional characters.

Liberate yourself from the shoulds and should nots.

Liberate yourself so that you may pour all your juices into the poetry of life that makes you feel more alive in your own dreams.

Liberate your voice

You have a story to tell. You have art to express. You have something to say. Are you using your voice the way that you feel intuitively called to? Or are you swallowing your tongue and keeping your mouth shut?

Your voice carries a specific tone and frequency that has a deep resonance with those who are meant to hear it. Your voice sends out a transmission that ripples through the world for others to be drawn to you. There is a little piece of them waiting to hear you to be able to connect with you. Are you willing to put your voice out in the world for others to hear?

When I speak of your voice in this section, I am speaking of both your verbal voice, and your written voice, and any other form of expression that is a part of your authentic voice.

Just as there are those who will deeply resonate with your voice, there are those who will be viscerally repulsed by the tone of your voice. This may be because of their own internalised conditioning and prejudice about who you are, or it may be that they are simply not aligned with you or your art. Either way it is important for us to recognise that we are not for everyone.

We cannot hold our art back in the fear that others will use their own voice to be loud about the ways they do not like what we create. Holding back your art out of fear for how others will react to it is holding back beauty from those who are meant to experience your art.

Some of your favourite authors have one-star reviews and criticism on what you would consider their best, most life changing books. I occasionally go and read some of these one-star reviews to remind myself of this and laugh at how much I disagree about what these reviewers are saying about the book. There are also times I completely agree with what the one-star-reviewers are saying, but the reasoning they are giving for disliking the book are some of the reasons I loved it. This is where 'negative' attention can shine a new spotlight for others, who will deeply resonate with your art, to find you.

There are movies that you absolutely loved that you feel are masterpieces, that the critics tore to shreds in their reviews. There are movies that were incredibly boring or offensive to you that the critics loved.

This can be said for every piece of art that the artist had the courage to put out into the world using their own voice. There is no piece of art that has a worldwide consensus that it is beyond any 'negative' reactions from some.

What resonates for you will not resonate the same for all.

The same goes for your art, in whatever form it takes.

We are all creative in different ways, and we all make art in different ways.

Let go of the need for recognition as a leading energy when sharing your art with the world. While there are some who are designed to thrive while being recognised, this recognition needs to be detached from your sense of self to feel free when creating. Liberate yourself from *needing* every piece of art you create to be revered by others.

Taylor Swift is one of the most celebrated, awarded, and successful artists of all time, yet she has many haters. She used this to her advantage early in her career, writing songs like Mean, and a lot of her Reputation album, but now she mostly ignores it (at least publicly). And she continues to create for the millions of people in the world who do deeply resonate with her art.

You can use the negative reviews and reactions to your advantage with your art as well, like sharing those one-star reviews if they actually list reasons others will love your book. There is a difference between someone having genuine dislike or criticism for your art, and those who simply want to spread hate on anything that shines brightly. Use your discernment in what to engage with, but never take any of it to heart or personally.

In liberating your voice you are not opening the door to spew whatever comes to your mind out onto others, with this liberation comes a refinement of what you do say as you are tuning into your authentic voice. There is just as much power in what you choose not to say, as there is in what you do say. Not everything you think needs to be heard by others, you giving consideration, kindness, and respect to others and determining they do not need to hear something you want to say is not swallowing your tongue. It is using discernment which is a high frequency gift. These thoughts do not cling to your mind until you blurt them out when triggered, you graciously let them go because you understand the power and impact of your voice the deeper you connect with it, and the more you allow your true voice to be liberated.

In the liberation of your voice, you are liberating a core piece of yourself, you are inviting more freedom into your body and in the way you express yourself to the world. This brings great flow to the way that you create your art, and also a deep sense of inner freedom with how and what you create.

The liberation of your voice is for yourself first and foremost, and it will have such beautiful and wide ripples into the rest of the world, especially through the lives of those you are meant to connect with through your art.

Liberating your voice makes you a clearer creative conduit for the cosmos, you channel in a way that allows you to express as a voice box for the universe, allowing the most divine art to flow through you.

Re-wild your inner child

If you have spent any time with young children, you will know that they are completely wild, unpredictable, at times destructive, and they are incredibly creative. Children are innately wild at heart as they follow their natural impulse to play.

Children who have the spaciousness of freedom in their lives have the space to be naturally creative. Without structure, the way that adults have structure, they are free to play and explore through their days, as they learn through experimenting. They have the space to make a mess and be oblivious to any judgement that may get projected onto them by adults who don't embrace their own wildness.

You have this child within you. Your inner child is meant to be wild, innocent, playful, curious, and above all, free to explore life like a playground. Your inner child lives within your heart as your living reminder to play and create.

There are times when you need to be an adult, but there are many times when you can embody your inner child to bring more joy and childlike play into whatever you are doing and whatever you are creating.

Osho says "become a child again and you will be creative. All children are creative. Creativity needs freedom – freedom from the mind, freedom from knowledge, freedom from prejudices."

Hardly anyone judges a child when they make a mistake while learning something new, they are given grace while they are learning and developing through their play. If there is judgement projected onto them, they do not take that into their play.

As you grew from your completely creative and innocent self into your teenage years and then adult self, you likely picked up some limiting beliefs and conditioning that created layers and masks, hiding or distorting parts of your true, most creative, self. The essence of you has always shone through but the expression of your essence likely didn't carry the pure wildness of your inner child's heart as you grew into an adult in the world.

The more you connect with your creative energy the more these little lost pieces of you will synchronically reveal themselves and integrate back into the whole of you.

The more you connect with your inner child the more you will remember the creative dreams you had as a child, and the forms of creative expression you were naturally drawn to. You will feel wild enough to pursue these things for the sake of enjoying the moment of play.

You may feel blocked creatively because you were bullied or berated for your expression as a child which in turn caused you to hide part of yourself from others. If this was linked to your natural creative expression then it could have in turn blocked all of your creative expression that made you feel light and playful.

In my first book Gentle Glow I told the story of how when in primary school I was the only person to not make it past the auditions into the school choir, which stopped me from doing two things that I loved to do for fun at the time – sing and write songs. I can admit that I am pretty tone deaf, and not what most would call a 'good singer,' but I do believe that if I was encouraged and helped to improve the skill of singing (and maybe even placed in the back row) I could have been good enough to blend into a primary school choir group.

We live, and grew up in, in a world where children are mostly discouraged from pursuing things that 'can't make them a living' unless they are exceptional, even then many would still be discouraged. The thing is, children like to play. They are not thinking about their future careers when they are playing around and even if they are it is ok for those dreams to be innocent imaginary play for the moment they are in.

This kind of conditioning domesticates us into the capitalist world that has us believing we cannot do anything that won't eventually lead to making us more money or having more things. Which is a bunch of bullshit. The irony is that pursuing creative play has so many benefits to your energy, radiance, problem solving, and enjoyment of life that it most likely will result in opening your field to more abundance.

This conditioning may have turned you into a bit of a bully towards your own inner child, shutting them down and calling them names whenever they gently try to suggest something fun. Give your inner child the tenderness and love they deserve and know their ideas are what brings joy and play into your life.

This is your time to undomesticate yourself, to re-wild your beautiful inner child, to pursue art just for fun and follow the journey for what it leads you into.

When you combine your childlike curiosity and playfulness, with your adult skills, resources, and knowledge – you pave the way for artful creative magic!

Your heroic journey

The Hero's Journey is a story you have seen play out many times across many different mediums. You know the story where we meet our unlikely hero who is suddenly forced to leave their normal life through some sort of crisis, and they find themselves in an unfamiliar world. In this new world they likely meet a friend, a mentor, an antagonist, and often a love interest. Through their story they face battles, they gain new skills and perspective, they connect deeper with their inner strength and wisdom, they often find gifts within themselves, they overcome the challenge posed by their foe, and they return to their normal life, forever changed.

This is the basic template for many stories including Harry Potter, Star Wars, The Hunger Games, Shadow Hunters, and many more. Sometimes these stories add magic, science fiction, fantasy, and other elements. Whatever the additional elements, the overarching story for our hero is already written.

The Hero's Journey was popularised by Joseph Campbell in his book, released in 1949, The Hero with a Thousand Faces. In Campbell's book he summarises this journey as - "a hero ventures forth from the world of common day into a region of supernatural wonder: fabulous forces are there encountered and a decisive victory is won: the hero comes back from this mysterious adventure with the power to bestow boons on his fellow man." In the book he breaks this down into 17 steps the hero will take in their journey.

In Nilims Bhat and Raj Sisodia's book Shakti Leadership, when exploring the Hero's Journey, they note "mythology is simply a very creative way to express human psychology."

Bhat and Sisodia explore the limitation of Campbell's work in that his examples are mainly about men. They quote an interview conducted by Maureen Murdock noting that Joseph Campbell told her that "women don't need to make that journey…all she has to do is realise she is the place that people are trying to get to." Murdock, like myself, did not find that answer to be reflective of the experience of feminine heroics, and she went on to write a book called The Heroine's Journey.

Bhat and Sisodia note that the key difference in the heroine's journey is that "when a woman quests and comes into her own inner source of love, she gains (that) freedom for herself." They note that while the hero quests for power to gain meaning, the heroine quests for love to gain freedom, and that each has different inner resources at their disposal throughout their quest. The hero has direction, logic, focus, confidence, and strength, to name a few. The heroine has surrender, intuition, radiance, sensuality, patience, and vulnerability, to name a few.

The heroine's journey is broken into five stages – a loss of power or violation, coming to grips with limiting beliefs, slaying the dragon of feminine inferiority, discovering the Shakti/feminine qualities within, and arriving at freedom and belonging.

The journey can be initiated through the forces of life, or by a conscious choice. This applies to both the hero and the heroine.

The differences between how the hero and heroine's journey have been depicted may seem stereotypical, but when tuning into how this all applies to you, look beyond the labels. Take the elements within each that resonate.

Whoever you are, you will take many heroic journeys through your life. Some will be bigger than others. You will meet a point in your life where you are either called to be the hero of your own story, or to find more depth within yourself.

Explore the stories, myths, and archetypes that resonate with you, the tropes or storylines you love to see play out again and again, explore how they are reflected in your own story or the story you wish to live.

Are you willing to go into the underworld to liberate your light?

Are you willing to slay the dragon to retrieve your treasure?

Are you willing to descend into darkness to unlock your gifts?

There is art in the story you live. You get to creatively fill the space within each of the steps you take. Even if the template of your story is already written there is so much space for your creative juice to paint the details.

Your creative impulse is calling for you to be the hero in your own story. To liberate yourself from being a side character.

The next step is yours to take.

Your multi-dimensional nature

You are a multi-dimensional being whose light is shining in many different colours, with light reflected in many directions. Just like a diamond, you came to be this way through pressure, in the diamond's case the pressure came from deep within the earth, in your case the pressure is coming from the impulse of evolution inside of you. With each turn you take, each challenge you rise through, and each time you meet your own depth; another face of the diamond reveals its light.

This is your time to liberate yourself from any labels, niches, language, anything at all, that attempts to confine your shine in one certain direction.

Use Taylor Swift's song 'Bejeweled' as your inspiration to let yourself shine as you naturally do when you are being your true self. A diamond cannot help but shine.

Know that the pressure you have experienced throughout your life is serving to your light. You get to choose what to pour your light into and it is ok if there is a wide range of things you feel drawn to throughout your life.

Liberate yourself from the mindset of 'this doesn't make sense for me.' Rather trust your creative impulse and follow it into all the ways that allows you to connect with your multi-dimensional nature.

Here is a poem I wrote for you to muse on here

You are drawn into the church
and arrive at the sacred altar
bowing in devotion
a devotion that does not falter.

The church is the temple
that holds your bones and blood
and the depth of your spirit
throughout your life force floods.

There is darkness through the voids
and glistening portals and light
there are paths of tribulation
there is bliss, ecstasy, and delight.

On your voyage to your core
immeasurable depth will be unearthed
upon your arrival to your radiance
in your true and deepest essence, you will be immersed.

In the pressure of the journey
many faces of iridescence are formed
on the magnificent diamond that is you
you will emerge transformed.

Your light will shine always
in many directions throughout all the land
as you follow your light within the dark
your inner diamond will grow and expand.

Creation as a spiritual practice

Creation is my God.

There is a liberation here if you currently have any kind of limitation around what spirituality, or your personal spiritual practices, need to look like.

In many ancient teachings there are said to be two paths to God. The path of meditation, and the path of love. The path of meditation pulls you away from the material world into silence and inner retreat, this gives rise to the image of the monks meditating in secluded temples. For some this path is the resonate direct line they find to God (or their own divine power). Even though they are removed from the world many monks pray for humanity and bring great lightness through the world. For many this path is unattainable, and it may be the reason their mind convinced them that spirituality was not something for them. The path of meditation can of course be practised to a less extreme, cultivating inner silence and your own inner pathway to God.

The path of love however takes you right into the heart of life, where you embrace the drama, the relationships, the despair and disappointment, the heartbreak, the mess, you embrace the full story of life while keeping your heart open to love. Your pathway to God could be found in your love for pop culture, soap operas, indulging in chocolate and wine, embracing pleasure, and all of the other juicy experiences you enjoy. The pathway of love is equally as spiritual as the pathway of meditation even though it is not widely viewed as such.

However you choose to practise your own spirituality and build your own relationship with God is no more superior than how anyone else chooses to. God is in all. When I speak of God, I mean any word that represents the divine oneness for you.

Osho says that "a creative person is one who has insight, who can see things nobody else has ever seen before, who hears things that nobody has heard before – then there is creativity"

Channelling from Spirit allows you to bring divine art through you onto earth, with that you bring insight and imaginary elements that have never been seen or experienced before. Even if there is something similar in existence, your creation will have something original and unique about it.

Julia Cameron shared multiple golden quotes in relation to creativity being a spiritual practice, the subtitle to her book The Artist Way is – a spiritual path to higher creativity. In this book she says -

"When we move out on faith into the act of creation, the universe is able to advance."

"Creativity is oxygen for our souls. Cutting off our creativity makes us savage. We react like we are being choked."

"Creativity is a spiritual practice. It is not something that can be perfected, finished, and set aside."

"In a sense, your creativity is like your blood. Just as blood is a fact of your physical body and nothing you invented, **creativity is a fact of your spiritual body** and nothing that you must invent."

It is a universal truth that your creativity is sacred in many ways, it is spiritual essence that has taken primal form.

In infusing your creative essence into all that you do, and in the way you give reverence to life, you allow it to be your spiritual practice.

There can be no liberation, without your creative energy.

Without the freedom for us each to individually create in flow with our own creative impulse, there is no freedom in the world. Without the expression of each of our creative energies, there is no liberation to set us all free.

Here lies a paradox, that there must be freedom for all for there to be freedom for one, *and* that our liberation comes through the freedom of one person at a time. Seeing through the paradox we can see that there is nuance and layers to the way we can look at freedom.

From a spiritual and divine perspective, we can see and feel everything in its divine timing, all beings exactly where they need to be right now in their own story lines.

From a more primal human perspective, we can see external factors that are keeping some from their own freedom. From this viewpoint it can be hard to comprehend how there could ever be liberated freedom for all.

In her book Big Magic, Elizabeth Gilbert says "just because creativity is mystical doesn't mean it shouldn't also be demystified — especially if it means liberating artists from the confines of their own grandiosity, panic, and ego."

Your creativity is sacred, divine, magical, impactful and gives way to liberation, AND you do not need to take it too seriously to think that you are any one's saviour. It is creation itself that will make way for liberation through you.

Without creativity there is only dry lifeless action going through the motions of life yet remaining on the same page in the story of life's evolution. Creative energy is needed for evolution, it is needed for our story to progress and expand. You are a reflection of the macrocosm in which you live, so the microcosm in which your creative energy sits is of vast importance.

Your creative energy is not really *your* creative energy. It is a fragment of creation itself sitting within and flowing through you.

Your creative expression is unique because you as a human are a differentiated expression of the divine whole. No one drop within the ocean is the same, yet all are part of the vast ocean, so too are you simultaneously differentiated and in oneness with the whole. As a drop of the whole, creation moves through you to evolve itself.

Without the story of you playing out within our collective world, there is no collective liberation.

Whatever you yearn for liberation from within your life, trust your creative impulse to illuminate the way forward. Know that your liberation is serving to the liberation of all.

Liberation through creation: summary

- Liberation is provoking you through life to be more of yourself and to be more creative.
- Allowing your energy to be in the present, rather than fixated on the past, allows all moments to be artful. Liberating yourself from your past creative work makes way for art you could never predict or plan to flow through you.
- Through life you have likely been conditioned to think you should want to create certain things or live in a certain way. When you liberate yourself from the dreams of others you give your creative energy the spaciousness it needs to create what you truly want.
- Your voice sends out a powerful resonance for others to connect with you, be inspired by you, and be impacted through your art.
- Your inner child is wild at heart, embracing this playfulness is magical for your creativity.
- You are on your own heroic journey, this story is the art of your life.
- You are a multi-dimensional diamond, reflecting light in many directions. No label could ever accurately detail the creative value you bring into the world.
- Creation is a spiritual practice as you embrace the path of love to connect with divineness.
- There can be no liberation without your creative energy.

CHAPTER EIGHT
YOU ARE A WORK OF ART

From your first breath of air, and every breath thereafter, your life has been destined for vibrant art as well as much laughter. Life is your canvas, get out your brush and colours to spread, go out and write the most amazing story that could ever be told or read.

Sacred Symbolism – the dove

The dove is seen as a messenger between worlds, strongly connected to both the physical world, and the world of spirit. In this sense they have a strong symbolic link to creativity, communicating with us what creation wants to take form, and taking messages from our creations into spirit.

Doves are creatures of both the earth and air, of the world and of the heavens, they are highly adaptable to many conditions as they accept wherever they find themselves to be. The dove appears to reveal spiritual insight, to direct you into harmony with the synchronistic flow of life, and to direct you inwards to your inner peace.

Doves are seen in the world as symbols of peace, purity, and innocence. They have a soft lulling coo that is calming and sweet.

Both male and female doves produce milk for their babies, they often starve themselves in preparation for their babies to be born, this ensures their milk is pure. This is symbolic of the pure innocent love we have for our young, in the dove it is primal and instinctual. Even their sacrifice is divine.

All acts of the dove are primal, yet these acts hold the essence of the divine.

The dove's life is a work of art, it doesn't need to plan it as so, it just is.

As is your life.

Differentiated through unity

There are around 8 billion people on this earth right now, each having a completely unique expression. There are billions more people who have been on this earth before us, and billions more who will be here.

Billion is such a big number it can be hard for our mind to grasp the magnitude. If we look at this number through time, one million seconds is only 11.5 days, whereas one billion seconds is 31.5 YEARS.

Out of the billions and billions of humans in existence across all time – you are unique and differentiated from all of them.

While others may look similar, you have a distinctive face.

No two people have ever been found to have the same fingerprints!

The sound of your voice is entirely unique.

Combine all these physical attributes with all your other features and your vessel is truly one in billions and billions. When you factor in all your inner qualities, you can begin to fathom just how rare you are.

Have you ever paused to ponder what created all these completely one-of-a-kind humans across all of time? Perhaps you have considered that there may be one Creator or God. You may have deemed there to be no divine-ness at all while arriving at the conclusion that everything happens by chance in a chaotic world. Maybe you have mused on the idea that we are in a simulated reality controlled by our future selves. There are many potential possibilities, and that is part of the fun! Revel in the mystery.

Whatever creative force you choose to believe in, even if you are still playing the field to form a strong belief, the very cosmic force that created billions of differentiated beings is flowing within you and wants to be expressed in the world through you. You are incredibly rare. You are a rare piece of art who gets to live in the world and create art in a way that only you can.

Even though you are different, you emerge from the oneness in which all differentiated expressions emerge. To come into our human existence we begin our story with a sense of separation, coming out of the void where there is only unity into the world where we appear to all be separate. This leaves us with this inner sense that drives us in our evolution back to the oneness that is within each of us.

This inner pressure has likely led you on an external journey to 'find yourself.' To find what makes you happy and fulfilled, what allows you to feel at peace. Through your external journey you likely had some incredible experiences, perhaps some turbulent ones too but these made you stronger in many ways. It is when you turn your journey inward that you will find the home you have been seeking for most of your life, you find this home in your heart within the frequency of love. All you have been searching for has been within you the entire time.

In going inwards you find the sense of belonging that you tried to find in other people. You find the unity within yourself as you tap into the cosmic energy that connects you to all life within the universe.

In this unity you remember more of yourself. In remembering more of yourself you connect more deeply than ever to your life-force, to your creative essence. You connect to the flow of creation that is moving within you and through you.

Paradoxically, it is within this sense of unity found within yourself that you become more of your differentiated self. Your art is reflective of this. In the oneness you allow the cosmic flow of creation fully through you, moving through your body you merge your unique essence with its expression.

"Art is the most intense mode of individualism that the world has known." – Oscar Wilde.

Your art is an expression of yourself in any given moment, it is your footprint in the world. Your legacy. Your art is forever lasting, whether it is seen or recognised at all. The only recognition your art needs is from you.

The divine drama of your life

Imagine the story of your life as an incredible TV show, one that captures the real essence of life – there is romance, comedy, tragedy, drama, and all your favourite things that you love to watch play out on the screen.

What season is currently airing?

Perhaps you are in season one of the reboot, or maybe in season 10 that is about to wrap things up before the spin-off, or maybe the solid season three.

Are there any flashbacks from previous seasons that you feel stuck in, like you can't move forward from the memory of them?

What is the overarching story arc for this current season?

What stories, themes, character development, and progression from previous seasons are showing up in this one?

Who are you as the main character? What has your character development entailed through previous seasons and the current one? What is so engaging about you as a main character? What are your character flaws that make you more lovable?

What character development would you love to see for yourself as the main character?

Is there a co-star or are you the solo lead?

Who are the supporting cast in this series?

What roles do these supporting cast members play in the plot of this season?

What cast members may need to make an exit from the show in order for the story of the main character (i.e., you) to progress?

Which cast members are the antagonists?

What previous characters should there be a reunion with soon? Perhaps a holiday crossover episode with someone who got their own spin off from your life a little while ago?

Which cast members could secretly be the antagonist?

What tropes are present? Any rivals to friends to lovers' stories taking place?

Does the current setting suit the vibe of the show?

What plot twist would you love to see?

Given the main character's current choices, conflicts etc. how do you see their story progressing through the series?

What would you love to see more of in the next episode?

What is becoming a little too repetitive in the series?

What are your favourite parts about the story this series is telling?

What would the soundtrack be like for this show? Would there be any laughing tracks needed?

If your future self was the narrator to this show, what kind of things may they be saying about your current choices?

There are so many different prompts to get your imagination painting the full picture of your life through the lens of a TV drama, you will likely think of more yourself. If TV shows are not a medium of art that you love, you can instead choose to think of your life as a book series, a movie, a play, even a painting, whatever medium of art you feel most drawn to.

In any of these you may not be in control of the setting, the overarching storyline, or much of the casting – but you have full autonomy when it comes to the script and much influence over your inner experience while living the story.

The overarching story may be already written, *and* there is so much space within the template to fill with heart and magic.

Your life is a work of art. Your entire life! From your greatest romance to the way you washed your dishes last night – every moment can be infused with your creative essence and turned into art.

This is a practice, and a devotion to fully living your life.

In this imagining of your life as a TV show, if someone else could be watching it, what may they highlight as an area where things have gotten a little stale or repetitive, what areas of your life may be calling out for some extra zest, and how you can make the most out of the storyline that you are currently living through? These are prompts for you to ponder.

When you take this somewhat objective big picture view of your life you can more easily see the things that you miss when caught up and lost in the detail.

The drama in your life is divine in the way it adds to the evolution of your story, it is part of the art in your life.

Drivers of your artful character development

If we stick with the idea of your life being represented by a TV show, there are always plot points that drive the development and growth of the main character.

These drivers could be any sort of conflict that they must navigate, facing off with their antagonist, heart break, or a twist that completely shakes their view of reality. These character development drivers are usually intense, and take our protagonist on a journey into their own shadows before arriving in their gifts and coming out the other side for their 'happy ending.' Of course, in TV shows these happy endings are often short lived before the central conflict for the next season is set up in a season finale cliffhanger.

In your actual life these drivers are what drive your evolution through your story, they may not be as fast paced and consecutively present compared to a TV show, but these events arise to help you grow.

There may be times where you find yourself repeating the same patterns, and the same mistakes, where you regress for a moment into your old mindset. I see commentary around this when it happens in TV shows, that some characters have had 'all their character development reversed'. I don't see it this way, it is a normal part of our story to at times revert back to old patterns, especially in moments where emotions are running high. As you unlock more of yourself you will navigate these regressions with more ease to ground yourself back into the evolutionary progress that you had previously made.

When exploring the challenges in your life right now, consider how they could actually be sacred drivers of your character development helping you rise, and ground, into more of yourself.

Is there an enemy who is actually a friend?

Is there a friend who is actually a rival plotting against you?

Is there a love interest who secretly loves you back?

Are there dynamics in your family that you want to begin shifting?

Are there relationships that need to end?

Your core challenges that drive your evolution will be found within your relationships, there can of course be other challenges you face but it is your relationships that give the sweet juice in your life. It is your relationships that play big, beautiful roles in your story and in the art that you create.

In Madelyn Moon's book, Artist of Love, she says "when you create, liberate, and express the vastness of who you are, you will fall madly, wildly and utterly in love. With yourself, and with others. You've unlocked the dam of truth, and what comes gushing out is rich with colour."

Your relationships give your life vibrant colour, including your relationship with yourself. Embrace the conflict, the intense emotions, the drama, the love, all of it, it is all driving you into yourself and through your story.

Interweaving storylines

When you let your art out into the world you interact with all the other billions of stories that are playing out around you.

Your art will be the muse for more art to be born.

A story I love about art inspiring more art is how a Taylor Swift song inspired the creation of a movie, and said movie inspired Taylor Swift to write another song.

The film Someone Great, directed by Jennifer Kaytin, was inspired by Taylor Swift's song Clean from her 2014 album '1989'. Jennifer Kaytin said in an Instagram post that she "found the most comfort in Clean, a song about rebirth after love lost. It inspired me and Someone Great."

The film then inspired Taylor Swift to write her song Death By A Thousand Cuts to include in her 2019 album Lover. It wasn't until after the release of her album that Taylor Swift found out that one of her songs was an inspiration for the film Someone Great in the first place.

Another amazing element of this interwoven inspiration is that Lizzo's song Truth Hurts was featured in the trailer and movie for Someone Great. This catapulted her into more mainstream success, sending a ripple for all of her beautiful creations to a wider audience too.

I see art inspired by Taylor Swift's art all the time, from clothing, music, portraits, books, videos, and so many other things being created all the time as a flow on from her creative expression.

In letting your art out into the world, you become part of the interweaving cycles of creation.

In Taylor Swifts' Variety Directors on Directors interview, when speaking on making more albums at a more rapid pace, as she has done in recent years, she said "the more art you create, hopefully the less pressure you put on yourself, if you stay ready you don't need to get ready, if you keep making stuff you just keep making stuff, and hopefully you get better at it… you don't have to belabour and polish the doorknob so long that you forget to open the door."

Let yourself put your art out into the world, for yourself, and also allow it to be a muse for others. You putting your art out in the world elevates the world into a more inspired state of mind, where more beautiful art will continue to flow and flourish.

When the world is in a more elevated inspired state of mind, and all the storylines continue to intertwine, more creation is not only inspired but also willed from others.

In an interview with Jimmy Fallon, Taylor Swift said "there is a part of it that I don't quite understand how it comes to fruition. There's something so mysterious about writing. But I found the more I write, the more I keep writing…the more things I make, the happier I am"

The mysterious part is that sometimes creation flows through us because of the way we are a muse for others. In Chapter One we explored how sometimes our creations are willed into the world through others, this is another magical part about allowing ourselves to be connected to all of these interweaving storylines. The more we create the more we inspire others to create, the more we inspire others to create the more we feel called to create. Let yourself be part of this magical cycle.

The script of life

The script is a powerful element when it comes to the experience of the overall story. Think of a TV show or movie that has an incredible concept, amazing actors and actresses, beautiful setting, and yet you just cannot get fully on board with loving it because the script feels cringy, forced, and out of place. In contrast, there are likely movies that do not have a lot going for it from the outside looking in, but the script, the writing, and the messages of the movie feed you in some way whether it is just really fun, enlightening, or entertaining.

The exact same scene could play with two different scripts which would create two entirely different pieces of art and experience within that plot point.

In the story of your life there are many elements in which you did not choose, the environment, family, and privilege you were born into, the state of society, and your genetic predispositions to name a few. There are perhaps many elements of your story that were written in the stars. There are of course choices and consequences in which you directed when it comes to your story but even those are heavily influenced by external circumstances.

This concept first dropped into my life through the work of Richard Rudd in my exploration and study of the gene keys, that we do not always get a say over the storylines that we live but we do get a say over the script.

We get to choose how we respond to moments that present in our story, rather than react and spiral. We get to choose our inner thoughts and perspective through story points in our life. We get to choose the level of poetry we weave into our words as we live each moment.

What may seem contradicting is that the script can at times seem to be a driver of the story, that the ripple effect of the words we use and the action we take can seem like it takes our story in different directions. The paradox we live in is that we simultaneously create the story of our life, while living the story of our life that has already been woven into the fabric of the cosmos.

Even if we were just puppets of the Gods, playing along to how they move us with string attached in their kinky little game with each other seeing what they can make us do, or if we truly were God materialised experiencing life through ourselves, or if we were some simulation from a future version of ourselves, all situations where we have no control whatsoever in how our story will progress, we still have autonomy in the present moment and choose how we will experience said moment. This is where the script comes to life, this is the only moment that we get to fully experience. This is the moment where we make art.

Maybe we never really create anything, maybe all art is predetermined and simply moves through us. Osho comments on the paradox that "the real creator knows that he has not created anything. Existence worked through him. It has possessed him, his hands, his being, and it has created something through him. He has been instrumental. This is the real art, where the artist disappears."

Again, even if this was the case we still get to play with the script in how we experience that moment of art flowing through us. Don't take the mystery of life so seriously that you forget to play while you live it.

Choose your script in each moment and have fun with it, make art with how you live and how you love.

Another poem I wrote for you to muse to

You are a character of the cosmos
Playing out your life on the great stage
The storyline may already be written
Each day the gods turn to a new page

Even though the cycles of stories continue
Using us to act out the inevitable end
There is a new beginning around every turn
That we act out again and again

We may not have control of the storyline
But as for the script we do have a say
Same goes for the love we bring to our role
And how we feel and breathe throughout our day

If our destiny is already written
Does what we do mean anything?
Do we keep embracing the theatre of life?
Is there anything of value that we really bring?

The point *is* to live
To love, to laugh, and to feel
Even if we have no control
We still decide to us what is real.

Living in the moment

In this book we explore creating with the intention to share with an audience, to sell, and to have a tangible end materialised creation.

We also talk about creating in the moment, making every moment a work of art.

In a life that is art, there is no distinction in value to the world between the two.

It may be hard for the mind to grasp but the way you decorate your room can be just as impactful in the world as your bestselling book. The ripple effect of each is something we will never be able to see or mentally comprehend.

This journey is about infusing everything with the beauty of your creative energy – this makes everything art.

Remember there is no pressure, there is nothing to prove.

Let yourself play, let life be your jungle gym or your favourite story ever told!

Practice creating in a way that you can hold no attachment to, like a mandala made with flowers and love – don't even take a photo of it, create it and then watch as the air takes it away. Sing a song in a moment and don't write down the beautiful lyrics that flow through you.

Know which moments are just for you to experience the beauty of, and trust your discernment to know which art you feel called to share.

Be present to the art unfolding in this moment, and in all moments.

Curating your inner art gallery

A new analogy for us to explore that has interwoven elements with all others is imagining your inner world as an art gallery. Perhaps this art gallery takes up your whole inner being, or just a building you can visit at times within yourself.

In this gallery you curate the art of your life.

Some pieces you create and hang proudly on the walls.

In other areas you may have an altar with portraits of your greatest muses and perhaps items that hold sentimental inspirational meaning.

Each room could have its own theme.

Each season of your life could have its own exhibition.

Each piece of art created and curated connects you to the beauty of life and stirs up more of your creative juice each time you visit this place within yourself.

Play with this idea and paint a picture in your mind for what you would have on display within your own art gallery, and how you would curate the space.

Each time you seek inspiration you will know where to find it within yourself.

You can externalise parts of your inner art gallery in devotional altar spaces in your home. Made up of pieces that bring joy, grounding and inspiration to your inner artist.

You can hang art on your walls that is reflective of what is on the walls in your inner art gallery. These physical anchors provide a devotional space for you to connect inwards. Of course you do not *need* anything external to the creative essence of your inner artist, but let yourself indulge in their wants. What art do you want on display in your physical home and within the home of your body.

Life as poetry

The more open to your creativity you become, the more poetic you naturally become. You start to see the poetry that exists in the way you get to live your life.

In Julia Cameron's book The Artist Way she speaks of 'shadow artists.' These are people who "often choose shadow careers – those close to the desired art, even parallel to it, but not the art itself." She shares that shadow artists find it incredibly difficult to recognise themselves as possessing creativity and that to them, allowing play in their life is hard work. I resonate with this from the time in high school that I decided to become an accountant. What I was really drawn to was business, being a leader in business, and while I wouldn't have used the word creative at the time, I was drawn to the creative decisions that business owners get to make. But I explored accounting so that I could understand business before having my own business, like anyone who undermines themselves I went to the adjacent middle step. Accounting is the skill of deciphering and translating the story that the numbers are telling, this did appeal to me, and I was good at it, but there was only so long I could stay in the work I was doing before my true desire to be in business myself created enough pressure to break me out of compromise, and into my real dreams.

Explore where you have settled in your own life, where you are acting as a shadow artist because some part of you believes you aren't creative, or good enough to be creating and working in the way that you really want to.

In breaking through the way I was settling, life became more poetic and freeing.

Osho says, "let your life be a painting, let your life be a poem."

And that "Nirvana is to live the ordinary life so alert, so full of consciousness, so full of light, that everything becomes luminous."

Elizabeth Gilbert says "a creative life is an amplified life. It's a bigger life, a happier life, an expanded life, and a hell of a lot more interesting life. Living in this manner — continually and stubbornly bringing forth the jewels that are hidden within you — is a fine art, in and of itself."

Carolyn Elliot says, "the whole universe is just God playing elaborate rounds of hide'n'seek with Godself."

Oscar Wilde says "man is least himself when he talks in his own person. Give him a mask, and he will tell the truth."

All quite poetic views on what it means to live and what it means to live creatively.

In his transmission for the 55th Gene Key, Richard Rudd says that "we are entering into an era of great beauty – it will be a transcendent era in which creativity will rule and life itself will be experienced as art."

Your life holds the poetry that you allow it to.

The greatest story ever told

Everywhere you look in life there are stories, from ancient myths to marketing campaigns. Stories are the fastest route in connecting someone to the core message of any piece of art.

The common saying goes that a picture tells the story of a thousand words. Imagine the magnitude of your life story when you read it frame by frame for all the pictures that could be captured throughout your life. You are living in your story at every moment.

Storytelling is reflected in all mediums of art, from books and movies, to paintings and songs, through to the gene keys, tarot, dance, pottery, and all else.

In the gene keys, the story goes from the shadow to the gift to the siddhi, not always so linearly.

In tarot the major arcana tells the story of the fool's journey until they meet the world ready to begin the journey again, but they are a different kind of fool when they begin their next story. One who now knows that they know nothing.

Stories allow us to deepen our poetic view of life, using symbolism, metaphors, and analogies, when simple words and sentences could never give the inner meaning we connect with our story true justice.

Your story is simultaneously a perfect, artful, masterpiece, *and* a beautifully messy work in progress. Let it be both. Live in this duality. Embrace it.

Let your life be the greatest story ever told.

There is no comparison needed when viewing your own story in this way, for your story is the only one that you get to live!

Your story is a masterpiece because of your creative energy, because of the art that you get to infuse into every moment, because of your primal and divine creative impulse.

Throughout this entire book you may be questioning what exactly your art looks like, what is it that you are already creating? The answer is – everything.

Everything you create is art because it has your creativity infused within it. Remember that your creativity *is* your life-force energy, it is always within you and flowing through you for as long as you are breathing. You may find times where it feels like the fire of this energy is almost out, but there are always embers still there burning and all you need to do is shift your attention to fanning them for the flames to burn and roar once more. Your creative energy is for you to make art through your great story, and to drive your evolution which in turn drives the beauty and evolution for all of humanity.

The art you share throughout your story is up to you. Always consider your intention for wanting to share any piece of your art, this becomes infused with the transmissions. Don't worry if you have doubts, or emotions are running high, you are a powerful force who now knows how to give these thoughts and feelings space to transcend while you don't take life too seriously.

Go out and live the greatest story ever told while embracing and nurturing your creative self. Tell your story in whatever medium you feel drawn to, keep redefining what being creative means to you, and continue reclaiming all the creative juiciness within yourself. You are more creative than my words could ever explain to you. Find this feeling within yourself and trust the wisdom that comes through your inner world.

You are a work of art: summary

- The more unity with the collective you feel within yourself, the more of your differentiated self you embody, and the more your unique flavour of creativity shines through.

- Imagining your life as a divine drama playing out on a screen can give new perspective to the artfulness present and the things that need to shift in the way you are living your story.

- All the conflict, drama, intense emotions, and challenges that you experience are for the evolution of your story.

- All creation muses on itself. Your art inspires more art which inspires more art which inspires more art, in a forever flowing cycle of creation.

- You may not have control over the storyline of your life, but you do get to choose the script in each moment that you live.

- Curate your own inner art gallery to draw inspiration from whenever you need.

- Be present to the art unfolding in the moment you are in, there is no distinction in value between the art you create and the art you live.

- Life is as poetic as you allow it to be. The more poetically you live life the more your creativity flows into the art of each moment.

- The greatest story ever told is the one that you are fully living.

FINAL WORDS

Creation is both a single emanation, and a tapestry of many elements. In the wise words of Maya Angelou "you can't use up creativity. The more you use, the more you have." You have an infinite sweet oceanic reservoir of creative juices inside of you, prompting and urging you to let it pour out and fill your life with art.

Your creativity is as much like fire as it is water. There are always embers burning deep within you, even if sometimes it feels like the fire is out know that you can fan the tiny flames to soon be a roaring fire again. Your creative impulse is equally primal and divine, the creative action and expression it guides you into is of sacred high service to the art of your life and the evolution of our collective humanity.

You are a creative being.

You are here to create.

Your art is beautiful.

Your highest art is in your true presence that you paint the world with. Simply being yourself adds beauty to the world.

Take all the lessons you have learned from this book as musings to contemplate on, let the lessons intertwine with your creativity and your own perspective and wisdom will shine through. Have fun as you play with any action you feel inspired to take.

Thank you for being here within the art of my writing, this book channelled through me for you.

My prayer for you

May you feel just how creative you are, in your blood, bones, and heart.

May you trust in your creative impulses, letting them guide you to make a start.

May you always sense the synchronicities and the abundance of time and space.

May you express yourself freely, liberate your voice, create at your own sacred pace.

May you know that you are worthy, that you are creative beyond any measure.

May you be willing to explore the full depth of life, the pain and all the pleasure.

May you embrace that you are Source manifested, that creation is part of you.

May you see that the beauty of your art is everywhere, in all you say and do.

May you know you are innately creative; this is definitively true.

May your creative story of evolution be one that you keep moving through.

May you live your life and create your masterpiece like everything is a work of art.

May you know you are within the cosmic web of creation; you are a divine part.

Acknowledgments

There are many people I wish to acknowledge and thank for being part of the journey in bringing Tapestry of Creation to life. Some were part of my journey in connecting more deeply to my own creative energy, becoming more expressive, and gaining clarity in the wisdom I wish to share. Others had involvement in this book without which this book would not hold the potency and power that it does. Others are my big life supporters who energise me with their love and presence. I give my love to all of these people, for there are too many to name.

Those who I feel need a permanent mark of thanks from me inside this book are:

My butterfly ideas for always filling me with so much excitement. If you have read the book you will know that I refer to creative ideas as energetic butterflies who love to flirt with you by whispering their stories in your ear. I am deeply grateful for all of the cosmic ideas who came to play with me through the creation of this book. This work of art channelled through me in many ways. I know that I cannot take sole credit as Source played such a big role in this book's creation.

Leesa, Marilyn, Alex, Lara, Bianca, and Chelsea, for being the first people I trusted inside the pages of this book while she was not yet in her final form. I loved sharing this writing with you and receiving your feedback and praise. You amplified the energy of this transmission in preparation for its birth into the world. Thank you for being friends that I hold and trust dearly.

Chelsea Todd, for being part of the above group, and going the extra mile to provide proof reading and your loving notes to bring even more potency and power to each passage inside this book. I appreciate your insights and your eye for detail.

Rachel Symington, for my work with her was a catalyst to me starting my podcast Depths of Creation, from the beginning of the podcast mid-2021 I planned out chapters that always had the intention of forming this book. While many elements have been expanded upon and evolved since the initial recording and transcription of my podcast, that experience kick started the foundation for this book.

Grigoria Kritsotelis for being a beautiful amplifier in my life. Whenever I am in her presence beautiful things always seem to follow. Many of my clients have found me through the light she has shone on my work which I am incredibly grateful for. Grigoria is constantly opening portals in my mind, the conviction in her voice when she shares her wisdom tends to lead me into deep contemplative musings. I am so grateful for all the ways we have worked together and for the friendship we have formed.

Richard Rudd for bringing The Gene Keys to life in his poetic transmission. His teachings have expanded my mind and opened my heart in many ways. I am incredibly grateful for the way he shares his wisdom with the world, and the framework he created that I have had the beautiful opportunity to share with many of my own clients. I hold deep reverence for all of this work along with the entire legacy and sacred roots of The Gene Keys, in Human Design, the I Ching, and all others facets that weave in.

Taylor Swift for being a genius storyteller whose artistry has been a beautiful muse for my creativity, my emotional depth, my creative expression, and for all of life.

All the artists and creators in the world who inspire me, especially the creators who I have referenced within the tapestry of this book. I appreciate their artistic expression immensely.

The beautiful clients I am honoured to work with. I have deep gratitude for all the amazing clients I have gotten to work with, my insights and wisdom are always deepened through their questions and our work together. I would like to give great gratitude to the women I was working with during the journey of writing this book. I would often feel very high on life and juiced up on creativity after our calls and other interactions which I used as fuel for much of my writing. You know who you are, and I love you dearly.

Thank you to my family and friends who listened to me talk about my upcoming book many times, even when you didn't fully understand what I was writing a book about, I appreciate you holding space for me to be excited while you were often the first to hear about my breakthroughs and developments. To my little almost three-year-old nephew Antonio, thank you for your wild checky-ness that the world needs much more of and showing me what it means to truly play and laugh. To my baby almost one-year-old niece Adriana, thank you for filling every room with joy every time you smile and reminding me to be present whenever you are near.

I would like to acknowledge and pay my respects to the Traditional Owners of the land in which most of this book was written, the elders past, present, and future of the Latji Latji people.

And finally, I must give acknowledgement and deep gratitude to you. Thank you for being here within the pages of this book. It has been a labour of love curating the elements of my wisdom and teachings for the story of this book. I am very grateful that you are here immersed in this art, and incredibly grateful for all the art that you express into the world. Even if I never see it, I feel it every day. You are a divinely creative being and don't ever forget that!

About the Author

Rachel White is an Australian author, speaker, coach, gene keys guide, and artist of life. The primary focus of her work is to connect women with their true essence and unique expression of sacred art.

Rachel has followed many creative impulses leading to a myriad of creative experiences, from creating her many online programs, live events, a virtual magazine, physical products, books, poetry books, kids' books, and more. Rachel draws on a rich tapestry of life experiences to activate women to connect with their creative impulse to bring to life whatever they feel called to.

Before pursuing her creative path, Rachel worked professionally as an accountant for eight years while volunteering in many organisations. Her work included a five-month secondment to New Zealand in 2015. It was in New Zealand that Rachel began to open spiritually, which was a catalyst to the work she does now. Upon returning home, Rachel completed her Life Coaching certification in 2016 and Yoga Teacher Training in 2017. In 2018 Rachel took the soul leap into her business and allowed more space for the full expression of her creativity.

Rachel draws on an inspiring depth of embodied study in spirituality, healing, personal growth, creativity, and The Gene Keys with an innate vision for seeing and nurturing others' gifts, to serve as a muse and channel for transformation. Rachel creates and dances through life as a work of art, and artfully guides her clients to live a sacred, authentic, divinely creative life.

Human Design – Manifestor
Gene Keys core gifts - Altruism (27), Totality (28), Anticipation (42), Leadership (31)

Connect with Rachel -

@byrachelwhite across any social media platform

On her podcast Depths of Creation

Or website www.byrachelwhite.com

More books by Rachel you may enjoy -

Wander: a complication of my thoughts about life, nature and people expressed through poem

Vineyard of Honey: poems

Living is Art: affirmations to remind you of the sacred, creative, intuitive, and incredible human that you are

References

Books

Richard Rudd (2013) *The Gene Keys: Embracing your higher purpose*, Watkins

Dr Libby Weaver (2017), *Rushing Woman's Syndrome: The impact of a never-ending to-do lust on your health*, Dr Libby Online Pty Ltd

Dr Joe Dispenza (2012) *Breaking The Habit of Being Yourself: How to lose your mind and create a new one*, Hay House

Julia Cameron (2021), *The Artist's Way: A spiritual path to higher creativity*, Souvenir Press

Madelyn Moon (2022), *Artist of Love: The modern woman's guidebook to unleashing her creativity, deepening her relationships, and becoming the leading actor in her own life*, Maddy Moon Inc

Carolyn Elliot (2020), *Existential Kink: Unmask Your Shadows and Embrace Your Power (A method for getting what you want by getting off on what you don't)*, Red Wheel

Osho (2000), *Creativity: unleashing the forces within*, Griffin

Nilma Bhat and Raj Sisodia (2018), *Shakti Leadership: Embracing feminine and masculine power in business*, Berrett-Koehler

Elizabeth Gilbert (2016), *Big Magic: Creative living beyond fear*, Bloomsbury Pb

Joseph Campbell (1949), *The Hero with a Thousand Faces*, Pantheon Books

Brene Brown (2013), *The Power of Vulnerability* [audiobook], Sounds True

Movies + TV Shows

Jared Bush and Byron Howard (Directors), *Encanto* [film] (2021), Walt Disney Animation Studios

Anthony Russo and Joe Russo (Directors), *Avenger's Endgame* [film] (2019), Marvel Studios

Sam Raimi (Director), *Spiderman* [film] (2002), Columbia Pictures, Marvel Enterprises, and Laura Ziskin Productions

Frank Coraci (Director), *Click* [film] (2006), Columbia Pictures, Revolution Studios, Happy Madison Productions, and Original Film

Penelope Spheeris (Director), *The Little Rascals* [film] (1994), Amblin Entertainment and Kingworld Filmed Entertainment

Robert Zemeckis (Director), *Back To The Future* [film] (1985), Amblin Entertainment

Jennifer Kaytin Robinson (Director), *Someone Great* [film] (2019), Feigco Entertainment, Likely Story, and I Can & I Will Productions

Robert Zemeckis, Jack Rapke, Jacqueline Levine, Jeff Rake, David Frankel (pilot), Joe Chappelle, Len Goldstein, Romeo Tirone (Executive Producers), (2018-2023), *Manifest* [TV series], Compari Entertainment, Jeff Rake Productions, Universal Television (2018–2021), Warner Bros. Television

Michael Schue, David Miner, Morgan Sackett, Drew Goddard (Executive Producers), (2016-2020), *The Good Place* [TV series], Fremulon, 3 Arts Entertainment, Universal Television

Music

Taylor Swift and Jack Antonoff (Writers), Taylor Swift (Performer), *Death By A Thousand Cuts* [song] (2019), on album Lover, Republic Records

Taylor Swift (Writer and Performer), *Cornelia Street* [song] (2019), on album (Lover), Republic Records

Taylor Swift and Jack Antonoff (Writers), Taylor Swift (Performer), *This Is Me Trying* [song] (2020), on album Folklore, Republic Records

Taylor Swift and Jack Antonoff (Writers), Taylor Swift (Performer), *Bejeweled* [song] (2022), on album Midnights, Republic Records

Taylor Swift (Writer and Performer), *Mean* [song] (2011), on album Speak Now, Big Machine Records

Taylor Swift and Imogen Heap (Writers), Taylor Swift (Performer), *Clean* [song] (2014), on album 1989, Big Machine Records

Taylor Swift, Jack Antonoff, Fred Fairbrass, Richard Fairbrass and Rob Manzoli (Writers), Taylor Swift (Performer), *Look What You Made Me Do* [song] (2017), on album Reputation, Big Machine Records

Taylor Swift and Liz Rose (Writers), Taylor Swift (Performer), *All Too Well (10 Minute Version) (Taylor's Version) (From the Vault)* [song] (2021), on album Red (Taylor's Version), Republic Records

Lin-Manuel Miranda (Writer), Jessica Darrow (Performer), *Surface Pressure* [song] (2021), on album Encanto (Original Motion Picture Soundtrack), Walt Disney Records

Olivia Rodrigo (2021), Sour [album], Geffen Records

Melissa Jefferon, Eric Frederic, Jesse Saint John, Steven Cheung, Amina Bogle-Barriteau (Writers), Lizzo (Performer), *Truth Hurts* [song] (2017), on album Cuz I Love You (Deluxe), Atlantic Records

Other

Alice George (2019), Smithsonian Magazine website, accessed November 2022, <https://www.smithsonianmag.com/smithsonian-institution/thank-world-war-ii-era-film-star-your-wi-fi-180971584/>

Britannica (2022), Britannica website, accessed November

2022, <https://www.britannica.com/biography/Vincent-van-Gogh>

Alix Spiegel (2012), NPR website, accessed November 2022, <https://www.npr.org/sections/health-shots/2012/09/18/161159263/teachers-expectations-can-influence-how-students-perform>

The Tonight Show Starring Jimmy Fallon (2022), Taylor Swift Talks Record-Breaking Midnights Album, Music Video Cameos and Easter Eggs [video], YouTube, https://www.youtube.com/watch?v=T2F4iP2ocBo

Variety (2022), Taylor Swift & Martin McDonagh | Directors on Directors [video], YouTube, https://www.youtube.com/watch?v=x8zfsf4azLo

Jennifer Kaytin (2019), Instagram website, accessed November 2022, <https://www.instagram.com/p/B1fthzAJeQd/?hl=en>

Dr Libby Weaver (2019), Food Matters Podcast episode 6: Hormone, Stress, Weight Loss and The Art of Managing it all with Dr Libby, accessed November 2022, James Colquhoun, <https://www.foodmatters.com/podcast/episode-6-hormones-stress-weight-loss-and-art-managing-it-all-dr-libby>

Marie Forleo (2014), The Mental Exercise That Can Turn Wishes Into Reality [video], YouTube, <https://www.youtube.com/watch?v=BJFJu-JP4m4>

Taylor Swift, Instagram story posted 16th November 2022

www.ingramcontent.com/pod-product-compliance
Lightning Source LLC
Chambersburg PA
CBHW020317010526
44107CB00054B/1878